CHRYSLER, PLYMOUTH & DODGE
STOCK CARS

First published in 1997 by Motorbooks International
Publishers & Wholesalers, 729 Prospect Avenue, PO Box 1,
Osceola, WI 54020-0001 USA

Motorbooks International is a certified trademark,
registered with the United States Patent Office

The information in this book is true and complete to the
best of our knowledge. All recommendations are made
without any guarantee on the part of the author or
Publisher, who also disclaim any liability incurred in
connection with the use of this data or specific details

We recognize that some words, model names and
designations, for example, mentioned herein are the
property of the trademark holder. We use them for
identification purposes only. This is not an official
publication

Motorbooks International books are also available at
discounts in bulk quantity for industrial or sales-
promotional use. For details write to Special Sales Manager
at the Publisher's address

Library of Congress Cataloging-in-Publication Data
Craft, John Albert.
    Chrysler, Dodge and Plymouth stock cars / John Craft.
    p. cm. --(Enthusiast color series)
    Includes index.
    ISBN 0-7603-0357-6 (pbk. : alk. paper)
    1. Stock car racing--United States--History.
2. NASCAR (Association)--History. 3.
Chrysler automobiles--History. 4. Plymouth
automobiles--History. 5. Dodge
automobiles--History. I. Title. II. Series.
    GV1029.9S74C73   1997
    796.72--dc21   97-13563

On the front cover: The years between 1969 and 1971
were the famous "Aero Wars" among the major automobile manufacturers. During this time, the nose of the car
was modified, and a wing was added, allowing the cars to
clock up to 200 miles per hour. Buddy Baker drove a Daytona for Cotton Owens during the Aero-wars. He won the
Southern 500 in 1970 in a day-glo #6 car just like this
one. This particular Daytona is on display at the Joe
Weatherly Museum in Darlington. *Mike Slade*

On the frontispiece: Fins were the rage in 1960 among
most American auto makers. Plymouth Furys came outfitted with a particularly fetching pair. This fin is part of
Richard Petty's 1960 Fury.

On the title page: The 1971 Charger was a very successful
race car. It also made a handsome street mount. Sleek
and stylish, the Charger was referred to as the Coke bottle
bodied car.

On the back cover: The most widely recognized Chrysler
stock cars surely are those that have been driven by
Richard Petty. This 1972 Dodge Charger sports Petty blue
paint and the familiar logos of his long-time sponsors.

Printed in Hong Kong through World Print, Ltd.

CONTENTS

FOREWORD

Though Ford Motor Company and General Motors cars have come to dominate the NASCAR ranks of late, there once was a time of greater automotive variety along pit row. From 1949 until the mid-eighties, cars of the Chrysler Motor Company (Chryco) played a major role on the NASCAR tour.

From the earliest races in the Grand National series, Chryco race cars took an important rank on the tour. Early NASCAR star Lee Petty scored the first win for Plymouth in only the seventh race of the fledgling NASCAR series, for example. Many more visits to victory lane were in the offing for Plymouth, Dodge and Chrysler drivers.

During the fifties, Chrysler 300 drivers so dominated the competition that for a time the financial health of the series was placed in peril. When "Letter Series" drivers like Tim Flock and Buck Baker won dozens of races, non-Chryco fans began to stay away in droves. It would not be the last time that Chryco drivers would go on a winning tear through the starting field.

In the sixties, Dodge and Plymouth upped the performance ante by rolling out an all-new Hemi-headed 426ci big block engine that churned out enough torque to tow Amarillo to Anchorage. The engine helped crown Richard Petty the "King of Stock Car Racing," while humbling the Ford and Mercury hoards. By the end of the sixties, Chryco race cars had sported pointy beaks and soaring wings that helped keep Dodge and Plymouth race cars a regular fixture in victory lane.

So fast were Hemi-powered comp cars that the NASCAR dons felt compelled to introduce the first iteration of the now-dreaded restrictor plate. When increasingly restrictive induction rules choked the life out of the fearsome Hemi, Mopar teams switched to wedge-headed big blocks and later to high revving corporate small blocks—even so, Dodge and Plymouth drivers continued to enjoy superspeedway success.

Unfortunately, changing corporate interests ultimately left the Dodge and Plymouth fans and drivers without support in the late seventies and by the middle of the next decade, Chryco stock cars had become but a memory in the garage area. It is in the hopes that those golden memories of Dodge, Plymouth and Chrysler glory will never be forgotten that this book was written.

CHAPTER ONE

PLYMOUTH TAKES THE LEAD
Lee Petty Sets the Stage

The date was October 2, 1949, and the place was Heidelburg Speedway in Pittsburgh, Pennsylvania. The event in question was a 100-mile (200 lap) race around the half-mile dirt track there. It proved to be a memorable affair. The fledgling National Association for Stock Car Automobile Racing (NASCAR) sanctioned the race held that day, and it was only the seventh such stock car event to take place in the new for 1949 series.

A driver named Al Bonnell was the fastest qualifier during preparations for the race and his "Strictly Stock" (the original name for the NASCAR series) Olds claimed the pole starting position with a hot lap of 61.475 miles per hour. Though Bonnell and his Olds were not destined for greatness that October day (he ultimately finished dead last) the race's ultimate winner was. And so, too, was the car line that driver had elected to campaign. The driver was a fellow named Lee Petty and his competitive mount was a 1949 Plymouth that carried the number 42. It

There once was a time when Chryslers were the hottest thing on the track. That was during the mid-fifties, when Karl Kiekhaefer's big white fleet of Chrysler 300s won just about every race on the NASCAR tour. Mike Slade

Lee Petty switched to a lightweight Plymouth midway into the inaugural 1949 NASCAR season. A short time later, he scored the first Chryco win in Grand National (then "Strictly Stock") history. Though far from fast, the little flathead six-powered car was able to out handle its rivals on the rutted dirt tracks of the day.

was the first stock car win scored by the North Carolina driver and the first NASCAR triumph for a Chrysler competition car in the series. It wouldn't be the last—for either Petty or Chrysler. Petty went on to visit victory lane a total of 54 times before hanging up his helmet and gloves. He and other Chrysler, Plymouth and Dodge drivers collaborated to win a grand total of 365 Grand National stock car events between 1949 and 1973. As you can see, Petty's winning performance was truly the start of something big.

Like all of the other cars on the starting grid at Heidelburg, Petty's Plymouth was absolutely stock. And that's just the way that Bill France, NASCAR's founding father, wanted things to be. The official racing book of the day was a brief one, page affair that in sum dictated the use of totally unmodified cars in the series. In point of fact, many of the cars that showed up for the eight races that made up the inaugural 1949 NASCAR season were so stock that they were driven both to and from the track on race days.

Petty's lightweight little Plymouth was no different in that regard. Based on the nimble little business coupe chassis, Petty's race car rolled on a 217.8-inch wheelbase and was powered by a stone stock 97 horsepower flathead six-cylinder engine. While not exactly a powerhouse, what the little two-door coupe lacked in ultimate velocity, it made up for in low weight and nimble handling. As history records, that is exactly why Petty had selected the car in the first place. Petty's first NASCAR outing had taken place at the very first NASCAR-sanctioned strictly stock car race in June of 1949. Race prep for that 150-mile dirt track event consisted mostly of persuading one of Petty's (perhaps gullible) North Carolina neighbors to let the Randleman native drive his 1946 Buick Roadmaster in the event.

Though Petty's Roadmaster was fast on the straights, it lumbered through the turns like a

A replica of the little Plymouth that Indy driver Johnny Mantz piloted to victory in the very first Southern 500 is today enshrined in the National Motorsports Press Association Hall of Fame in Darlington.

wounded rhino. That trait ultimately led to a spectacular series of flips on lap 105 of the 197 that made up the race. It was THE first recorded racing accident in NASCAR history. The shunt put Petty out of the race and off of racing big heavy cars like the Buick. Shortly after the race (and the return of his neighbor's crumpled car) Petty vowed never to field a heavy vehicle in competition again. Three races later he showed up with a lithe, little Petty Brothers sponsored Plymouth and promptly finished seventh at the fourth ever NASCAR stock car race, held at the famed oval in Langhorne, Pennsylvania. Petty scored his second top ten finish at NASCAR event six in Martinsville (a second) before notching his already reported first "Strictly Stock" win in Pittsburgh.

Petty finished up his first season of stock car racing with a second at North Wilkesboro and wound up second only to Red Byron in the first ever seasonal points competition. It was a

As incredible as it sounds, the Plymouth that won the very first Southern 500 in 1950 had served as Bill France's "go-fer" car during the week before the race. A set of truck tires helped the street legal race car tame the Lady in Black. Mike Slade

promising start to a long racing career and one that caused other drivers to sit up and pay attention to the performance of Petty's diminutive Plymouth. It wasn't long before more cars from the Mayflower division began to show up on stock car starting grids all across the country.

Plymouth win number two came in September of 1950 at a soon-to-be-famous paved oval in a South Carolina town called Darlington. Opened just in time for the 1950 racing season, the new 1.25-mile banked superspeedway in Darlington was one of the first paved race tracks in the country. The inaugural race for the new track was

scheduled for the Labor Day weekend and organizers referred to the event as the Southern 500. A $25,000 purse was posted for that very first Southern 500 and, coupled with the high speeds made possible by the track's banked surface, it attracted scores of drivers. When the green flag fell, fully 75 stock cars roared off into the first turn. In that number was a West Coast driver named Johnny Mantz who had been saddled with the sobriquet "Madman Mantz" during his Indy car days. Mantz's competition car for the event was a rather unimposing-looking Plymouth coupe that had served as an errand runner during the days just prior to the race. NASCAR president "Big" Bill France, chief starter and flagman Alvin Hawkins and mechanic Hubert Westmoreland were listed as co-owners of Mantz's Plymouth. Even so, the car was anything but a pre-race favorite and, in fact, qualified dead last for the race with a hot lap of just 73.460 miles per hour. Though down on speed to the rest of the field, Mantz had a plan for victory that was based on his open wheel paved track experience. Mantz knew that 500 miles of competition would take the measure of most of the stock passenger car tires of the day, so he opted to mount harder compound truck tires under his light little #98 Plymouth. It proved to be a savvy move. Once the green flag fell, Mantz maintained a steady if somewhat sedate pace. Soon other drivers began to experience repeated tire failures (Red Byron experienced no fewer than 24 flats, for example) while Mantz continued to motor around the track without interruption. By lap 50, Madman Mantz had put his little Plymouth out in front of the rest of the field and that's just where the car stayed for the rest of the 400-lap event. Mantz's post-race trip to victory lane at Darlington would not be the last one made by a Chrysler driver after a Southern 500.

Plymouth drivers continued to visit victory lanes on the circuit through the 1952 season. Lee Petty was the most successful of the lot and he racked up wins at Hillsboro, North Carolina; Rochester, New York; Morristown, New Jersey; Macon, Georgia; and Langhorne, Pennsylvania. Herb Thomas took time out from his Hudson Hornet driving duties to score a Plymouth win at Martinsville, Virginia, in 1950 and at Macon in 1951 to round out Plymouth's stock car wins at ten for the 1949 through 1952 seasons. As things turned out, it would be seven more NASCAR seasons before a Plymouth would spend time in a Grand National victory lane. But that didn't mean that Mopar fans were left with little to cheer about during the interim. Not by a long shot.

Dodge Out in Front

The dawning of the 1953 Grand National season brought with it a wholesale defection of drivers from the Plymouth ranks. Fortunately for Mopar fans, that shift in driving allegiance was an "all in the family affair" for the most part that saw drivers like Lee Petty switch to cars of the Dodge persuasion for 1953. The reason for that shift was the all-new "Red Ram" Hemi engine that became a regular production option in the Dodge line that same year. And what an engine it was.

Though Chrysler Corporation had first unveiled a hemispherically combustion-chambered OHV V-8 engine in 1951, it was not until 1953 that the new and promising high-performance engine was assigned to duty in anything other than a "luxo-land yacht" Chrysler. In Dodge trim, the new engine was referred to as the "Red Ram." The new Dodge engine displaced 241.3 cubic inches and featured an over square 3.44-inch bore and 3.25-inch stroke. The cast iron cylinder heads that reciprocating assembly was nestled under were cast with true hemispherical combustion chambers and fitted with generously proportioned (for their day) valves. Street Red Ram V-8s were factory rated at a modest 140 horsepower. But it's certain that racers like Lee Petty were able to coax significantly more ponies out of a race-ready Hemi since the engine was fairly dripping with potential. But that potential was only available for Dodge (and Chrysler drivers) in 1953 since the Plymouth line was denied access to Hemi power that year. Hence, the wholesale shift to Dodge by Plymouth drivers.

The Dodge chassis of choice for drivers on the tour was the two-door Coronet hard top. Stretched over a 114-inch wheelbase, the redesigned for 1953 Coronet line weighed in at just short of 3,500 pounds and featured rounded, if unremarkable, bodywork. Like the lithe little Plymouths that Lee Petty and Johnny Mantz campaigned in previous seasons, the Hemi-powered

Dodges that showed up for the 1953 NASCAR season were smaller and more nimble than the lumbering behemoths that GM and Ford (Fomoco) drivers were forced to field. That fact, coupled with the power potential of the new Hemi engine, made a Dodge stock car circa 1953 a formidable package, indeed. And that's just what Lee Petty proved in spades at the very first race of the new Grand National season.

Palm Beach Speedway in sunny Palm Beach, Florida, was the site of the 1953 season opener. The race held there in February of that year was a 20-lap affair around a half-mile dirt track. Lee

Petty was on hand for the event and he qualified his Red Ram motorvated Dodge seventh on the field. When the flag fell the early laps were dominated by Hudson Hornet drivers. But by lap 49 of the 200 that made up the total, Lee Petty had muscled his Dodge into the lead. That's just where it remained for the balance of the race. When the dust (literally) had settled, Petty had turned a 60.220 miles per hour average speed into Dodge's first ever Grand National stock car victory. And so it was that the driver who'd claimed first blood for the Plymouth division in the NASCAR ranks also notched that same honor

This is the view that most competitors had of a Mercury Outboards sponsored Chrysler 300 in 1956. Team drivers like Buck Baker and Tim Flock won an incredible 30 races that season. Sixteen of those triumphs came in a row! Mike Slade

A Petty Plymouth was pulled around the track by a 97 horsepower flat head six-cylinder engine. Though that sleepy little six was far from a record breaker in the power production department, its lineal ancestors were soon striking fear in the hearts of Brand X drivers on the Grand National tour.

for Dodge. Making Petty's win even sweeter was the fact that Jimmie Lewallen claimed second place in the Petty Engineering 1952 Plymouth that was also fielded by the team that day. Petty's triumph was but a harbinger of the racing glory that would ultimately be won by Hemi-powered Grand National stock cars in the years to come.

Petty went on to score wins at Richmond, Martinsville, Shreveport and Spartanburg in 1953. Jim Paschal claimed a second Martinsville win for Dodge and along with Dick Meyer added top ten finishes in the Southern 500 to the Dodge tally of top performances that year. Petty and

Paschal's win came on dirt at short track events that made up the bulk of the 1953 NASCAR schedule. When the season was over, Petty's five wins and 25 top five finishes had earned him $18,446.50 and second place in the seasonal points chase (to Herb Thomas' Hudson effort). He was destined to improve on that performance the following season.

Chrysler Dominates

Chrysler race cars had been a presence on the NASCAR trail since the very first Strictly Stock race in 1949. Chrysler win number one came in

A stock bench seat, dash and controls confronted Plymouth drivers like Lee Petty in 1949 and 1950 on the NASCAR tour.

1951 at one of the most anticipated races staged that season. The event in question was dubbed the Motor City 250 and was held at Michigan Fairgrounds in August. Just staging the race was a major coup for Big Bill France and the NASCAR series, and it coincided with the 250th anniversary of the city of Detroit. When France got wind of the gala that city fathers had planned for the occasion, he quickly suggested a motorsports event featuring the same makes and models that rolled off of the nearby UAW assembly lines.

When race day arrived, just about all of Motown's movers and shakers had turned out for the dirt track affair that featured one circuit of the one-mile fairground course for every year of Detroit's existence. Fifty-nine cars qualified for the field and there were no fewer than 15 different makes of cars on the starting grid. In that number was a 1951 Chrysler driven by Tommy Thompson that had qualified fifth just a tick or so off of Marshall Teague's pole winning 69.131 miles per hour Hudson hot lap.

Though Teague's Hudson had dominated qualifying, by lap 25, Thompson had nosed his Chrysler into the lead. Curtis Turner hotly contested the point with Thompson for the bulk of the remaining laps (in his unfriendly, fender rubbing way) and on several occasions both he and Thompson slewed off the track in a shower of dirt and dust. But Thompson was not to be deterred and when the flag fell he roared across the line first. Chrysler executives at trackside that day no doubt left the fairgrounds with a bit more swagger than when they'd arrived. Lee Petty gave those same executives even greater bragging rights three seasons later when he won the first Grand National manufacturer's title for the Chrysler Corporation (as well as his own first driving championship).

Petty's championship season began with a third place finish at the season opener in West Palm Beach, Florida, where he campaigned a new Dodge. By the time the tour rolled into Daytona two weeks later for the famed beach race, Petty had swapped mechanical allegiances to the Chrysler line. The car he towed to Daytona from North Carolina was a San Juan Motors sponsored #42 New Yorker Deluxe that was powered by a 235 horse Chrysler Firepower Hemi. In 1954 trim the hottest corporate Hemi displaced 331ci and mounted an all-new four-barrel carburetor. Though compression ratios were kept low (7.5:1) by the factory, the engine was rated an industry high 235 horsepower. When installed in a 125.5-inch wheelbase, 4,000-pound New Yorker chassis, impressive performance was just a stab of the throttle away. And that's just what Petty provided at Daytona.

In the days before Bill France opened his banked superspeedway, stock car racers duked it out at Daytona on a 4.1-mile long oval that consisted of a sandy beach straight and paved surface street back stretch tied together by two sweeping sand-packed corners. Then, as now, the race at Daytona was the most prestigious on the tour. Petty signaled his arrival on the beach with a pole winning qualifying speed of 123.4 miles per hour. When the green flag fell, Petty quickly translated his horsepower advantage into the lead. Petty's primary competition during the race was Tim Flock's 1954 Oldsmobile, and in fact, it was Flock's #88 car that crossed the finish line first. That victory was a short-lived one, however, as NASCAR tech officials disqualified Flock when a post-race tear down turned up illegally polished carburetor passages. As a result, Lee Petty was awarded the win.

Petty followed up on that first place finish with a string of top five finishes after Daytona. Petty alternated between his Dodge and Chrysler race cars at those subsequent races and it was in a #42 Chrysler that he notched his second win of the year in a 100-mile event at Sharon, Pennsylvania. Chrysler wins at Rochester, New York;

Grand Rapids, Michigan; Charlotte, North Carolina; Corbin, Kentucky; and Martinsville, Virginia, brought Petty's win total to seven. Coupled with the 24 total top five wins Petty turned in 1954, those first place finishes made him the Grand National champion that season. As things turned out, that championship season was not to be the last for either Petty or cars of the Chrysler persuasion.

During the off-season, Chrysler executives decided to up the performance ante by unveiling an all-new luxury high-horsepower car called the Chrysler 300. So named because of the 300 horse Hemi engine that came factory stock in every iteration of the marque, the Chrysler 300 quickly became a legend on NASCAR tracks all across the country. In fact, Chrysler 300 drivers were so successful the next two Grand National

Street clothes and "washable" racing livery were fixtures on the 1949 NASCAR tour. And so was a young fellow from Randleman, North Carolina, named Lee Petty. Though Petty had begun the season at the helm of a GM car, he soon switched mechanical allegiances to cars of the Plymouth persuasion. That move turned out to be the start of a very long and rewarding association. Daytona Speedway Archives

seasons, they caused many a sleepless night for Big Bill France.

You see, NASCAR's sanctioning officials have never been fond of race cars that steal the show. And that's because it's been the show that's packed the grandstands since the inception of the series. The possibility of one car or make of car winning the majority of races on the circuit is not an inviting one for race promoters and sanctioning officials alike. Though the fans of one particular driver or marque may wish for an all-conquering season and wins at every stop on the tour, there's little doubt that the equally fervent fans of the also-ran teams would quickly lose interest in the series and spend their discretionary income elsewhere.

Close competition and "pro-wrestling like" driver rivalries keep ticket sales high and local track owners happy. Consequently, the sanctioning body has felt little compunction in modern times about "tweaking" the official rules book in the name of parity on the track. Restrictor plates, spoiler rules and body template requirements have all been used in the modern era to keep things nearly equal once the green flag falls. But it wasn't always that easy for folks like competition director Gary Nelson to bunch up the racing pack. That was especially true in the mid-fifties, when the stock cars that duked it out every weekend were just that—stock. During those days, when any given manufacturer produced a stock car that possessed superior performance to that of the rest of the field, there really wasn't much that NASCAR could do to keep that car from winning and winning and winning. And that's just what happened during the 1955 and 1956 Grand National seasons.

As mentioned, the cars in question were Chrysler 300s and the reason behind their dominance during the 1955 and 1956 seasons was a fellow named Carl Kiekhaefer. Kiekhaefer was the owner of the Mercury Marine outboard engine company and a hard-nosed businessman who knew how to make a buck. Far from being a racer or even a fan, Kiekhaefer was rather just a businessman looking for a way to advertise his wares in 1955 when he decided to jump into Grand National stock car racing in a big way. When market research identified the typical NASCAR race as a gathering place for potential Mercury Marine customers, Kiekhaefer was literally off to the races.

The first step he took upon setting up his 1955 team was to select cars from the 1,725 examples of Chrysler's new "Letter" series built that year as the basis for the effort. That choice was a natural one since the all-new 300s were literally the fastest street-legal American made cars of the day. Designed from the start with racing in mind, the new 300s were two-door versions of the normally sedate New Yorker line that had been treated to a mechanical dose of steroids. Rolling on revised underpinnings, designed to produce greater cornering resolve, and powered by Hemi-headed 331ci versions of the Chrysler Firepower V-8, the new cars were formidable machines.

Kiekhaefer's next task was signing a team of drivers. Reaching deep in his pocket, the Mercury executive decided that only the best would do, and soon he'd hired a number of the top drivers on the tour. In that number was 1952 series champ, Tim Flock.

Though Kiekhaefer didn't sign Flock to drive for the team until just days before the Daytona Beach race in February of 1955, Tim outpaced the rest of the field during qualifying to secure the pole position of that race with a speed of 130.293 miles per hour. During the race proper it was pretty much all Flock and his #300 Chrysler as that duo lead the race from start to finish. Fellow 300 driver Lee Petty finished in second with his Petty Engineering car to make it a one-two sweep for the Letter series' competition debut.

Flock went on to win no fewer than 18 poles and a matching 18 Grand National races during the 1955 season. Top five finishes in 14 other events earned Flock both $37,779 in winnings and his second Grand National championship. It was an incredible season for Kiekhaefer, to be sure. The grand total of 27 Chrysler wins notched by Flock, his fellow Mercury Marine drivers Speedy Thompson, Norm Nelson and Lee Petty had to be encouraging to both Kiekhaefer and Chryco executives. But Kiekhaefer wasn't satisfied with the results, and he redoubled his efforts during the off-season by signing Buck Baker and Frank "Rebel" Mundy to drive for the burgeoning team in 1956. Later that year, he also added Herb Thomas to his list of drivers, making the Mercury Marine operation truly a dream team.

Kiekhaefer's racing preparations left little to chance. In addition to fielding both the best drivers and fastest cars, Kiekhaefer also employed a team weatherman to predict track conditions on race day and he even hired scientists to take dirt track soil samples to help in selecting just the right tire and chassis combination.

In a first for the series, in a day when many competitors simply flat towed their race cars to and from the track, Kiekhaefer equipped each of his teams with a "box-type" truck and a wealth of spare chassis and engine parts. Kiekhaefer's teams also spent more than a little time testing their team cars in advance of a race, and drivers were required to keep track of engine and chassis performance during those sessions for analysis in post-test debriefing sessions.

Kiekhaefer's thoroughness in the preparation department extended to renting an entire hotel for the team to stay in during the days leading up to a big race. Bed checks were made to make sure that his strict curfew was enforced, and he sometimes required that drivers and their spouses stay in different rooms to keep pre-race "distractions" to an absolute minimum.

Kiekhaefer's military-like discipline and advance planning paid off, as mentioned, in 1955 with a total of 22 NASCAR wins and the series championship. With Baker adding to the talent pool in 1956 the team won just about every race they entered. The first race of the season actually took place in November of 1955 at Hickory, North Carolina. Tim Flock won that event convincingly in his #301 Chrysler leading all but 16 laps of the race. Buck Baker notched his first 300 win at the fifth race of the season in Phoenix, in a similarly dominating fashion. When the series rolled into Daytona, Flock made it two in a row on the beach course when he won from the pole and led all but two laps of the event. All told, Kiekhaefer's team Chryslers won an incredible 30 of the 50 features they entered. At one point during that historic season, team drivers won an unbelievable 16 straight events. By year's end, Baker had secured Kiekhaefer's second straight NASCAR crown and the team had won more than $70,000 in prize money.

Unfortunately for Kiekhaefer, his teams' on-track success did not translate into the fan goodwill he'd hoped for. In fact, NASCAR spectators took to throwing bottles at team cars by the middle of the season and some stayed away from the track altogether. Big Bill France was equally displeased with Kiekhaefer's success. With gate receipts in jeopardy, France had his tech inspectors tear down Kiekhaefer team cars and inspect them for any rules violations. When none were found, all France could do was hope the cars would break. And that didn't happen with any great regularity.

The 300Bs that Buck Baker and his co-drivers used to romp through the 1956 competition were all second generation members of the vaunted "Letter" series that had debuted in 1955.

For 1956, Chrysler engineers turned up the underhood heat a notch further by offering a 354ci, high-compression version of the hemi-

Lee Petty won the 1954 running of the fabled Daytona Beach race in this Hemi-powered Chrysler New Yorker. As you can see, stock cars were pretty darned stock in the days when Ike was still in the White House. Note the factory bright work that is still in place and the huge chrome bumpers that most cars of the day carried. Daytona Speedway Archives

spherically headed Chrysler Firepower engine that was rated at 355 horsepower. Built on Chrysler's marine assembly line, these engines featured forged internals, solid lifter, long duration camshafts and twin Holley carburetors. When installed ahead of a heavy-duty three-speed manual transmission and working with the upgraded suspension componentry common to the letter series line, these engines afforded spectacular performance, as Kiekhaefer's NASCAR opponents found out to their dismay.

Beyond the obvious steps taken to remove street-legal dead weight such as running lights and sound deadener, the 300Bs that Buck Baker and others drove in 1956 were disconcertingly stock. Kiekhaefer's race cars all carried the same side trim, fender badges and roll-up windows that they and the other 1,102 1956 300Bs had originally received on the Chrysler assembly line.

Things were much the same in the control cabin, too. Seating consisted of a stock bench that had lost its passenger's side seat back. The factory dash panel was augmented with a brace of analog gauges. The stock truck-sized steering wheel was retained unchanged as was the spindly looking column shifter. The most rudimentary of roll cages

Karl Kiekhaefer was serious about winning races on the NASCAR tour and he spared no expense in that pursuit. The Chrysler 300 teams he fielded were the class of any starting grid they graced. In a day when most drivers flat towed their race cars to and from the track, Kiekhaefer outfitted his teams with transporters and a staff meteorologist. And yes, the Grand National tour did make a road race stop at Road America in 1956! Daytona Speedway Archives

was relied upon for safety, and a single, quick release lap belt was all that kept Baker and the other team drivers from sliding wildly about the car's interior. The most notable racing changes made to a 300B's ergonomics were the deletion of carpeting and the removal of the rear seat. Another more subtle modification was a hole cut in the passenger side floorboard just behind the right front wheel. When a strobe light mounted nearby was turned on, it allowed the driver to see how much tread was left on the critical right front tire—an important bit of information in days when treaded street tires served double-duty on the race track.

The factory stock theme was followed fairly closely both under hood and under car in keeping with the NASCAR rules book. Suspension components were beefed up and extra shock absorbers were used, but overall, Kiekhaefer's cars had a lot more in common with regular production Chryslers of the day than do the current crop of silhouette stock cars running on the Winston Cup circuit.

It's been said that Kiekhaefer was more than a little surprised at the way the fans received his team's racing success. The respect and goodwill he had hoped to generate for his outboard motor company by competing in NASCAR was most definitely not forthcoming. And so, he folded his racing operation and left the stock car circuit as abruptly as he had entered it in 1957.

Lee Petty campaigned Hemi-powered Dodge Coronets in 1956, and the two wins he scored when added to the nine other Dodge victories recorded that season helped bring the total number of Grand National wins notched by Mopar drivers to 33. An impressive number indeed when one considers that figure represented fully 60 percent of the 56 NASCAR events contested in 1956.

Unfortunately, 1956 turned out to be the high-water mark of the decade for Dodge, Chrysler and Plymouth drivers in the fifties. By the time the next season rolled around, Fomoco and General Motors had elected to get involved with factory-backed NASCAR competition in a big way.

The high dollar contracts their arrival on the scene ushered in, were accompanied by a number of high horsepower mechanical packages, such as Ford's supercharged 312 engines, Chevrolet's fuel injected small block and Oldsmobile's J2 Rocket motor. The combined effect was more than even the most avid Mopar supporters could resist. Even Lee Petty swapped mechanical allegiances to General Motors for 1957. As a result, it was to be two long years before a Plymouth driver would visit a NASCAR winner's circle again and yet still another season before a Dodge driver would make that same trek. Chrysler's next (and final) NASCAR win took even longer to come about and didn't make it into the record book until 1961. Though Mopar fans found little to cheer about during 1957 and 1958, better days were just around the corner.

1959 "Fin" Cars Take Flight

NASCAR's first decade ended on a positive note for Chryco fans. That's because 1959 was the year that Lee Petty returned to the Plymouth fold after his dalliance with General Motors. The car that lured him back to the Mayflower division was a finned Sport Fury that was powered by Plymouth's new for 1959 361ci, 305 horsepower wedge motor. Interestingly, Petty didn't make that switch until the twentieth race of the 1959 season and only after winning the inaugural Daytona 500 in a 1959 Oldsmobile. The race that put Petty back in a Plymouth took place in June at Atlanta. Pre-race qualification for that 150-mile dirt track affair placed Petty far towards the back of the pack in thirty-seventh. Yet when the race was over Petty had bested the rest of the 40-car field to finish first. At least that was the way

things finally turned out, since at first it appeared that Petty's then unknown son, Richard, had crossed the line first in one of his dad's hand-me-down Oldsmobiles. When the elder Petty protested the result, a post-race reexamination of the scoring chart reversed the order of finish, handing Petty and Plymouth the win. Petty backed up that performance with a second Plymouth victory just four days later (again on dirt) at a hundred miler in Columbia, South Carolina.

Petty added five more notches to Plymouth's win belt for 1959 on his way to a second Grand National driving title. In addition to the $49,219 in winnings Petty pocketed that season, another high point had to be the emergence of his son, Richard, as one of NASCAR's rising stars. The younger Petty's performance in the Southern 500 brought particular distinction when he led the event early (in a Plymouth identical to his dad's) and then went on to finish fourth—outpacing his dad and many established stars in the process.

Papa Petty went on to score four more "Fin car" wins in his 1959 Fury and three more top five finishes. When coupled with his first of the season Oldsmobile finishes, Petty's Plymouth work earned him a then unprecedented third Grand National driving championship.

The first full decade of NASCAR, sanctioned stock car racing produced a total of 58 Chrysler wins, 20 Dodge triumphs and 17 Plymouth visits to victory lane. In addition, Chryco drivers had claimed the NASCAR championship four times. Though Chrysler drivers had but one more GN win waiting for them in the following seasons, for Dodge and Plymouth drivers, the best was yet to come.

CHAPTER TWO

THE SIZZLING SIXTIES
Birth of the Hemi

When the 1960 season dawned, the NASCAR series was on the cusp of dramatic changes. Though rough-and-tumble dirt track events had been standard fare for stock racers in the fifties, by 1960 Bill France and Curtis Turner had opened banked (and paved) superspeedways in Daytona and Charlotte, and yet another was slated to open in Atlanta. Those paved palaces of speed, coupled with the well-established superspeedway in Darlington, signaled an unmistakable trend towards asphalt racing and much higher speeds.

Lee Petty and son, Richard, continued to campaign big finned Plymouths for 1960, and that was the season that the yet to be crowned "King" of stock car racing would make his first trip to the winner's circle. Young Richard signaled that he was going to be a season contender at the Daytona 500 where he translated a nineteenth place starting position into a third place overall finish—one position ahead of his dad.

Richard Petty's "finned" Plymouths had picked up their soon-to-be-famous electric blue paint schemes by the 1960 NASCAR season. Petty started that season by finishing third in the Daytona 500. By the sixth race of the season, young Richard had scored the first of what would be 200 career Grand National/Winston Cup victories.

25

The control cabin in Petty's 1960 Fury was still mostly stock. A production-based bucket seat kept the future King in close proximity to the stock dash and three on the tree shifter. An oscillating-style house fan provided a bit of air conditioning during muggy summer events in the Deep South.

Fins were all the rage in 1960 among most American auto makers. There's even the chance that their soaring fins helped a bit in the handling department. Plymouth Furys came out-fitted with a particularly fetching pair. Richard Petty made them take flight at tracks like Daytona and Darlington.

27

As in 1959, the cars that Petty Engineering fielded had started out on a regular production assembly line as Golden Commando powered Sport Furys. In stock trim those cars stretched out over a 118-inch wheelbase chassis that rolled on torsion bar/"A" frame and leaf spring/live axle underpinnings. When stripped for oval track duty, the cars weighed in at just under 3,400 pounds. The raised block, 361ci wedge motors that powered Petty Engineering Plymouths for 1960 came factory rated at 305 horsepower and race-ready produced 325. That package was capable of speeds in excess of 145 miles per hour at Daytona in 1960, and by season's end had generated eight wins and 37 top five finishes for the two-car team.

Win number one for both Richard Petty and the 1960 Petty Enterprises effort came at the sixth race of the season. The site of that event was the Charlotte fairgrounds and the race there consisted of 100 miles around a half-mile dirt track. Young Richard qualified his Fury seventh for the race and kept race leaders in his sights until the closing stages of the event. He passed race leader Rex White for the top spot on lap 183 and kept his Blue and White #43 car out in front until the checkered flag fell 17 circuits later. Petty's purse

Dodge drivers in the early sixties campaigned Polaras. Though afflicted with novel styling, full-sized 1962 Dodges were plenty fast. Unfortunately, their Plymouth and GM rivals were a tad faster. Though the 413ci Max Wedge engines they carried into battle churned out an advertised 380 ponies, the Pontiac's SD 421 was good for even more.

was a meager $800, but even more rewarding days at the track were, of course, just around the corner.

Lee Petty notched his first 1960 season win at the next stop on the tour in North Wilkesboro, and Richard got one win closer to his ultimate total of 200 less than a month later with an asphalt triumph at Martinsville in the Virginia 500. Though Petty's first Darlington win was still in the future, he did turn in a second place finish (to Joe Weatherly) in the Rebel 300 and a sixth in the Southern 500. Richard scored his third and final win of the 1960 season in a 99-mile dirt track event at Hillsboro, North Carolina. When the dust and asphalt had settled at season's end, Richard Petty had finished the season second (behind Rex White's Chevrolet) in the points chase with dad Lee four places further back in sixth. Dodge drivers were not as fortunate and managed just one GN win for 1960 while Chrysler fans had nothing to cheer at all that same year.

1961 saw Chryco wedge engines increase in size to 383 cubic inches. The extra displacement resulted in increased under-hood heat, and for 1961, the hottest wedge motors were factory rated at 330 horsepower. Unfortunately, that increase was not enough to hold off the

Top of the line power for 1962 was the 413 Max Wedge motor. In street trim, that engine carried twin four-barrel carburetors and cranked out 380 horsepower. More cubic inches and an all-new set of Hemi heads were just around the corner for "RB" Mopar big blocks in 1962.

Though the race cars that Plymouth drivers campaigned in 1962 were as challenged in the styling department as their Dodge stablemates, they were able to out score them 11 to zero (in terms of Grand National wins).

ever-increasing number of factory backed Ford and General Motors drivers. Though both of those car manufacturers were supposed to be honoring an Automobile Manufacturers of America ban on factory-backed motorsports competition, the back door at both factories was wide open, and the special high performance parts that flowed through those portals went straight to the track—the NASCAR track, that is.

Unfortunately for Chryco fans, the most spectacular event of the season for Plymouth drivers was a career-ending, two-car shunt in the Daytona 500 that catapulted Lee Petty and a Chevrolet driver outside of the track in turn four. Though

Petty returned to the series after a long period of recuperation, for all practical purposes, the three-time champion's racing career as a driver came to an end in a smoking heap that day at Daytona. Son Richard's 1961 tour at Daytona didn't go much better, as his own Plymouth took an off-track and over-the-wall excursion during a qualifying race that knocked him out of the 500 itself. Richard did bounce back to score two short track wins for Plymouth later in the season, but on the whole, 1961 was an off year for Mopar fans on the circuit.

Things didn't get much better the following two seasons. Pontiac drivers had the hot ticket in 1962 with their Super Duty 421 wedge-powered

Catalinas. Pontiac executives had decided to go racing in earnest in 1961, and opted to make a special big block 421ci engine an "over the counter" option in order to legalize the package for stock car competition. That engine became a regular production option in 1962. Chryco engineers tried to counter with a hogged-out version of the 383 that displaced 413ci inches. Based on the Raised Block (RB) engine family, the new Max Wedge 413 was rated at 410 horsepower and no doubt cranked out a few more ponies in full race tune. Though the new big block was quite successful in NHRA drag race competition, it proved to be less than a match for either the 421 Poncho motor or Chevrolet's really fine 409 big block in NASCAR circles.

The 1962 season opened with a big win for Pontiac at the Daytona 500, where the legendary Fireball Roberts bested all comers in a Super Duty powered Catalina that had been prepared by Smokey Yunick. In a display of mechanical domination that none had seen before, Fireball claimed the top starting spot during qualifying with a hot lap of 156.999 miles per hour, and then went on to win both his pre-race qualifying race and the 500 itself. One bright spot for Chryco fans was Richard Petty's second place finish just 27 seconds behind Roberts' black and gold Pontiac. And that's just the way Petty's 1962 season wound up—in second place to a Pontiac driver. Though the soon to be "King" had turned in eight short track wins with his 413 powered Belvedere, it was Poncho driver, Joe Weatherly, who sat atop the points standings for the Grand National title. Three other wins scored by Mayflower division driver Jim Paschal in the second Petty Engineering Plymouth brought team wins to 11 on the season. Dodge drivers had another dismal season and failed to win a single event.

In an effort to answer the Pontiac and Chevrolet power advantage, Chryco engineers broke out the boring bar during the off-season and widened the corporate big block engine to a full 426 cubic inches. Horsepower increased to an advertised 425 ponies. It was hoped by all in the Mopar fold that the extra grunt afforded by the new engine would be the ticket to victory lane and the Grand National championship in 1963. And it might have been were it not for a couple of new 427ci racing engines unleashed by the competition that same season.

The all-new big block engine unveiled by Chevrolet for 1963 was shrouded by so much mystery that in time, teams on the circuit took to calling it the Mystery Motor. After tiring of being "whupped" by their Pontiac corporate cousins, Chevy engineers set out to devise an all-new, race-only engine for the 1963 NASCAR season. Topped with polyangle valved, free flowing head castings and featuring a beefy, four bolt main journaled block, the new engine churned out well in excess

Dodge drivers got back in the habit of winning Grand National races in 1964. The all-new 426 Hemi engine turned out to be the key that unlocked the door to victory lane for Dodge drivers like Anthony Joseph Foyt that season. A.J. drove a Ray Nichels prepped Polara to victory in the 1964 Firecracker 400 at Daytona, for example, with the help of Hemi power. Author Collection

of the 427 horsepower that Chevrolet modestly claimed for it. So promising was the new power plant that a number of former Pontiac drivers like Junior Johnson jumped ship and built Impalas. And though the new Bow Tie mill was far from being a regular production option (only 48 total Mystery Motors were ever built according to Smokey Yunick), NASCAR officials deemed it legal for competition.

Ford rolled out a new 427 of its own in 1963, too—and a new, more aerodynamic Galaxie body to race it in. Unlike the Mystery Motor, though, Ford's 427 was an actual production power plant that was based on the 406 FE big block engines that had been raced the year before. That having been said, the big incher Fomoco engine was far from being a sedate station wagon puller and in race trim was capable of cranking out in excess of 425 ponies for 500 miles at a time. Which is what Tiny Lund proved at the 1963 Daytona 500, where he drove a Wood brothers prepped #21 Galaxie to victory in the event. Junior Johnson set a new qualifying record to capture the pole of the 500 (with a hot lap of 165.183 miles per hour) and he and fellow Mystery Motor driver Johnny Rutherford captured both of the pre-race qualifiers to make speedweek's headlines a Chevrolet or Ford affair in 1963.

Chryco introduced the awesome Hemi, in part, as a response to Fomoco's high revving 427 wedge motor. The 1964 season's results left little doubt that the Ford motor was no match for the all-new hemispherically combustion-chambered motor.

Richard Petty finished sixth in the 500, making him the highest placing Chryco driver, but he was never a factor in the event's outcome. Petty took steps to right that wrong by winning the next two events on the schedule at Spartanburg and Weaverville, but Chevy and Ford drivers continued to be the "big dogs" on the 1963 superspeedways. At year's end, Petty had recorded 14 short track wins and 16 other top five finishes. An impressive performance to be sure, but not enough for a national title, which for the second year in a row was snagged by Little Joe Weatherly (who drove Pontiacs and Mercurys in 1963). Petty's stats did earn him a second consecutive second place

points total, and coupled with teammate Jim Paschal's Plymouth wins, brought Mayflower division triumphs to 19 for 1963. Dodge drivers were locked out of victory lane again on the NASCAR tour. That fact and many others would be radically changed in just one more season.

Birth of the Hemi

The 1962 and 1963 NASCAR Grand National seasons taught Chrysler engineers that more would be needed to win stock car championships in the sixties than a Max Wedge motor was capable of providing. And so it was that a team of engineers including Willem Weertman,

In street trim, Chryco's 426 Hemi often came dressed in dual four-barrels. It was a large and attractive power plant with valve covers suitable for basting a turkey in.

Race Hemis were limited to just one four-barrel fuel mixer. For 1964, that induction system made possible an "advertised" 405 horsepower: more than enough to win the Daytona 500 and just about everything else worth winning that season!

Tom Hoover, Bob Roger and Don Moore set out to build a world beating big block engine during the winter of 1962 and 1963. Their goal was to have the new engine up and running in time for the 1964 Daytona 500. That goal above all others dictated making use of as many pre-existing engine castings as possible. The decision to retain the already race proven block casting developed for the Max Wedge 426 was, therefore, a natural. Keeping the planned engines the same basic dimensions as the pre-existing 426 wedge motor was also a choice that was dictated by the project's incredibly tight time budget. Cylinder bore centers were accordingly kept at 4.80 inches and the engine was designed to maintain a 4.25-inch stroke and 3.75-inch bore yielding 426 cubic inches of displacement. Those decisions having been made, Weertman's team set out to design an all-new induction system that was capable of taking on all comers on the NASCAR tour.

The combustion chamber configuration of choice was a familiar one for the old-timers on the new engine team. Tom Hoover and Bob Rarey are given credit for the ultimate choice made, but in truth, the decision to build a Hemi-headed version of the 426 RB engine can actually be attributed to the engineers who perfected that design in the early fifties. With combustion chamber configuration and valve layout established, the other bits and pieces of the new engine package quickly fell into place. By early 1963, the foundry process needed to produce the engine was under way.

The first 426 race Hemi assembly took place the last week of November 1963—just two short months before speedweek 1964 in Daytona kicked into gear. Dyno testing of the new engine took place in December with more than promising results. When horsepower figures exceeded the 400 maximum that were registerable on the in-house dynamometer, a bit of slide rule work by engineers yielded a gross horsepower figure in the 425 range. Keeping in mind that that figure represented only the starting point of a race Hemi's ultimate horsepower potential, you'll easily understand the great deal of optimism that Hemi team engineers had about the coming Grand National season.

But all was not perfection with the new engine. In fact, as late as January 28, 1964, the Hemi engineering team was struggling with a cylinder cracking gremlin that suggested serious durability problems for the engine under racing conditions. The team literally worked around the clock to solve the engine's teething problems. Incredibly, the factory-backed teams who were slated to campaign the Hemi at Daytona didn't ultimately receive their engines until just days before the race. But when those engines arrived, they were ready to race—and win!

Qualifying for the 1964 500 got under way on February 7, 1964, and all eyes were on the Dodge and Plymouth teams as they queued up for their turn at two hot laps around the 2.5-mile banked track. Paul Goldsmith was one of the first Hemi drivers to pull out onto the track, and two laps later his Ray Nichels prepped Plymouth Belvedere had shattered the old track record of 160.943 by nearly 14 miles per hour! Richard Petty proved that incredible velocity was no fluke just a few moments later when he rocketed around the track at 174.418 miles per hour, just five-tenths of a mile per hour slower than Goldsmith's record shattering speed. The Ford and GM teams who watched

qualifying trackside must have felt like condemned prisoners just strapped down in the electric chair. Truth be told, they truly were doomed.

When the green flag fell at 12:30 p.m. on February 23, 1964, fans in the stands knew they were about to see something special take place out on the track. Goldsmith led lap one of the event before handing off to Petty. Bobby Isaac in a second Ray Nichels prepped Hemi car (a Dodge) mixed it up with Petty and Goldsmith for

To call the 1966-1967 Belvedere line boxy is an exercise in understatement. Characterized by sharp edges and 90 degree angles, the car was less than optimally aerodynamic. But who cares about air flow when you have a full race Hemi to punch holes in the air with? Mike Slade

Next
Richard Petty earned the title "King of Stock Car Racing" in this 1967 Plymouth Belvedere. Though it was essentially the same car he'd campaigned the year before, for 1967, the car was just about unbeatable. At one point during the season, for example, Petty visited victory lane at ten straight events. Mike Slade

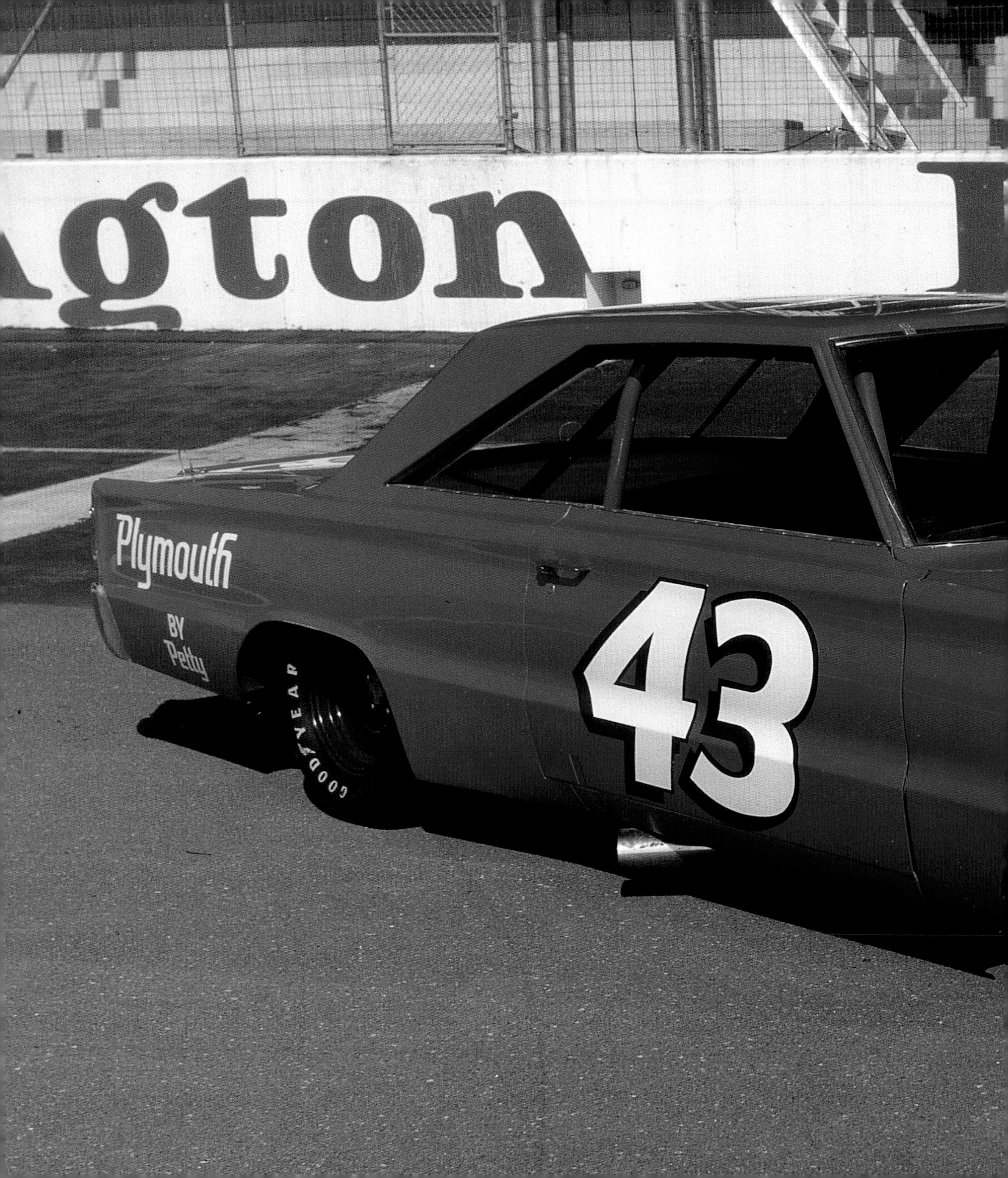

gton
Plymouth
BY
Petty
43
GOODYEAR

Dodge Polaras didn't get much slicker in the years that followed, but they did get a whole lot faster. That was especially true in 1964 when, along with their Plymouth counterparts, Dodge drivers picked up 426 Hemi engines. Pictured here is David Pearson's 1964 Cotton Owens' prepped Polara. Daytona Speedway Archives

a few laps and A.J. Foyt, driving a Banjo Matthews Ford, clawed his way to the front for two laps. Save for those two interruptions, the race was all Goldsmith, Petty and Hemi. In the end, Petty's #43 Belvedere crossed the stripe one full lap ahead of his closest rival, fellow Plymouth driver Jimmy Pardue. All told, Hemi Plymouth and Dodge drivers claimed four of the top five finishing positions. It was an impressive first outing for the new engine. And one that promised great success in the coming season.

The Hemi's all-conquering debut at Daytona also caused more than a little grumbling about it's non-regular production status—mostly from the Fomoco teams it had well and truly trounced. In time those complaints would grow in quantity and volume until the point that NASCAR officials were forced to take action. But not before Petty and his Hemi compatriots ran away with the 1964 Grand National season.

David Pearson scored the first Grand National win recorded by a Dodge driver in three seasons when he piloted his Cotton Owens prepped Coronet to victory in the Richmond 250, one race after

Daytona. He backed that up with a second Dodge Hemi win two weeks later in Greenville, South Carolina. Pearson won again at Hillsboro in April at yet another short track and Plymouth partisan Petty raced to a win at a hundred miler in South Boston, Virginia, one month later.

Jim Paschal came out on top in the grueling World 600 at Charlotte in May in his #41 Petty Engineering Plymouth. It was the second superspeedway win for a Hemi car in 1964 and Paschal's four lap margin of victory was a sign of just how bulletproof and dominating Chryco's new engine really was.

LeeRoy Yarbrough added his name to the Mopar winner's list with a victory at Greenville, and Buck Baker notched another win for Dodge at Valdosta in June. A.J. Foyt earned some bragging rights for USAC drivers at Daytona in July when he piloted a Ray Nichels prepped Hemi Coronet to victory in the Firecracker 400—a race that saw Hemi-powered cars sweep the top six finishing positions. Buck Baker won his third Southern 500 in August at Darlington in a Ray Fox Dodge and, as in the Firecracker, his Hemi car's only competition that day was the four other Hemi Plymouths and Dodges that crossed the stripe just behind him. Even long "retired" team owner Cotton Owens got on the Hemi bandwagon with a Dodge win at Richmond in the Capitol City 300 in September.

By the end of the incredible 1964 season, Dodge and Plymouth drivers had won 26 of the 62 races contested that year. The cars that made all that success possible were lightweight unit body repetitions of the Plymouth Belvedere and Dodge Polara car lines. The trim little Plymouths were the lightest and smallest of the pair and rolled on a 3,225-pound (street weight), 116-inch wheelbase. Torsion bars, reinforced "A" frames and a quartet of shocks were used to provide suspension movement at the bow, while a corporate live axle, parallel leaf springs and another double duo of shock absorbers were used to bring up the

Lee Petty's driving career was cut short by a wreck he had in the 1961 Daytona 500. It started in turn four when Petty's #42 Plymouth became entangled with Johnny Beauchamp's Chevrolet. Both cars ultimately catapulted over the top rail of the track and plunged into the parking lot outside. Petty's car was demolished and he was in the hospital for a number of months afterwards. Author collection

Richard Petty's 1963 Belvedere was fast—but not fast enough to beat the special motored Pontiacs he had to run against that season. Relief was just one season away. In 1964 Petty's Plymouth was to be powered by a full race 426 Hemi engine. Daytona Speedway Archives

rear. Special heavy-duty hubs (full floaters at the rear) were used all around, and they carried heavy-duty, fully metallic shoes and drums to help scrub off speeds.

A Dodge Polara carried a bit more weight and stretched out over a 119-inch wheelbase. Even so, a race-ready 1964 Dodge still tipped the scales hundreds of pounds lighter than a Holman & Moody Galaxie. Light weight, coupled with superior horsepower, has always spelled racing success. So the dominance displayed by Plymouth and Dodge drivers in 1964 shouldn't come as a big surprise.

Plymouth and Dodge drivers that year took in the rapidly passing trackside scenery from within a disconcertingly stock control cabin. A single factory-based bucket seat served as the central focus in both cockpits and that perch was encapsulated in a fairly rudimentary (by modern standards) roll cage. A stock but gutted dash panel carried a brace of aftermarket gauges just ahead of the stock steering wheel and four speed floor shifter.

Most regular production Plymouth and Dodge race cars circa 1964 were the class of every

starting grid they blessed, and they won just about everything in sight.

All told, Richard Petty made eight trips to victory lane and turned in a total of 37 top five finishes that earned him his first Grand National driving championship and $114,771.45 in winnings. David Pearson's eight wins and 29 top five finishes in his Cotton Owens Dodge gave him a third overall berth in the seasonal points race. Both Petty and Pearson would go on to win other Grand National driving championships and more than a few races for Plymouth and Dodge teams in the future. And most all of those wins would be earned with the help of the incredible 426 Hemi racing engine that first roared to life in 1964.

1965 The Hemi's Bellow Is Silenced

But none of that future greatness was destined to take place in 1965. And that too was a result of the 426 Hemi engine. As mentioned, Fomoco teams were none too happy with the sudden and immediate success enjoyed by Dodge and Plymouth Hemi teams in 1964. Their displeasure was based on the portion of the official NASCAR rules book that required a certain number of "units or models" to be produced in order to be legalized for Grand National competition. Fact of the matter was, a Hemi fan in the stands at a typical NASCAR race would have been hard pressed to find a regular production Hemi car on sale down at his local dealership. There just weren't any made (and wouldn't be until 1966). Access to "over the counter" Hemi engines was also pretty doggone limited too, unless you happened to be named Petty or Owens or Nichels.

Folks at Ford began to make noises about building a decidedly non-regular production Hemi-headed single overhead cam version of their 427 engine for use in 1965 at about the same time that some drivers took to complaining about the significantly faster speeds, characteristic of races in 1964.

Early word on the new Fomoco Cammer engine was that power production topped 600 ponies. That calculated amount of power promised to push superspeedway speeds well into the 180s, even when saddled with the bulk of a Galaxie chassis. Chrysler executives, jealous of the competitive advantage their new Hemi had earned in 1964, wasted little time in rising to meet the new Ford menace. Their theory was that if one overhead cam was good (as in the SOHC 427 Ford motor), then two just had to be better. Bill Weertman, Tom Hoover and many of the engineers who'd contributed to the original race Hemi project went back to the drawing board and penned an all-new set of dual overhead cam equipped, hemispherically chambered cylinder head castings that flowed better. Four valves per cylinder were part of the new head program as was an eight runner intake manifold. With Gilmer belt-driven cams acting directly on valves (in modern motorcycle engine fashion), the new engine was capable of more than 10,000 reliable rpm. Awesome horsepower figures were projected for the Chryco cammer, with some estimates exceeding 900 ponies in race trim! Best of all, like the original 426 Hemi, the new hemi heads were designed to simply bolt onto the existing 426 RB long block assembly.

NASCAR executives were well aware of the two new overhead cam engines that were coming down the pike. And they were equally aware of the complaints that many drivers were beginning to make about the much faster racing speeds on the 1964 circuit. When notorious leadfoots like Junior Johnson and Fred Lorenzen began to voice their concerns, Bill France just had to sit up and listen.

Big Bill's response to driver complaints and the escalating Fomoco/Mopar horsepower war was announced on October 19, 1994. It came in the form of four new rules that would govern competition for the 1965 season: 1) Engine size was limited to 428ci and the engine was required to be of a production design. 2) Hemi-headed engines and Ford high riser head castings (a set of non-production wedge castings that Ford teams had been allowed to use in 1964) were outlawed. 3) Cars legal for superspeedway competition had to carry a 119-inch wheelbase. A 116-inch wheelbase was permitted for short track competition. 4) Carburetion was limited to a single four-barrel that carried 1 11/16-inch throttle bores.

The news about the new rules hit Plymouth and Dodge teams like a thunder clap. In one fell swoop, both the race-proven 426 and the proposed dual overhead cam hemi were sidelined. Worse yet for Plymouth drivers, their lithe little Belvederes had been banned from the high banks for 1965 no matter what engine they elected to run.

The rules were slated to go into effect on January 1, 1965, just in time for the Daytona speedweeks that season. Chrysler executives were dismayed. Chrysler's Bob Anderson lamented, "Racing has always prided itself on being progressive. Here we are backing up." Racing Chief Ronnie Householder went further and said bluntly, "The new rules NASCAR announced have put us out of business down South." Ten days after France announced the new 1965 rules, Householder made an announcement of his own on behalf of Plymouth and Dodge factory-backed NASCAR teams. It read in significant part: ". . .[U]nless NASCAR rules for 1965 are modified or suspended for a minimum of twelve months to permit an orderly transition to new equipment, we have no alternative but to withdraw from NASCAR sanctioned events and concentrate our efforts in USAC, NHRA and SCCA. . ." And so it was that 1965 was the Grand National season that never was for Chryco teams on the tour. Richard Petty built a Hemi-powered Barracuda drag car called the 43 Jr. and David Pearson went quarter miling in Cotton Owens' drag race Dart dubbed the "Cotton Picker."

When Ford teams swept the first 13 places in the 1965 Daytona 500, France eased up a bit on the across-the-board Hemi ban and said that he'd let them run "If Chrysler makes a production line Hemi that is optional equipment for Plymouth Furys and Dodge Polaras." But Householder would not back down. The Moparless season progressed and with each passing race, track attendance decreased. Soon race promoters were raising a hue and cry and more than a few heated phone calls were made to NASCAR headquarters in Daytona Beach, Florida.

France's response to the pressure was to meet with USAC president, Henry Banks, to hash out a uniform set of rules for stock car competition in both racing organizations. It was a face-saving way for France to back off of his Hemi ban without having to publicly cave in to Householder's intransigence. The resulting NASCAR/USAC rules changes were announced in June of 1965. They established a minimum weight formula of 9.36 pounds per cubic inch of displacement; they permitted the still non-production Hemi engine to be raced in Polaras and Furys on tracks longer than a mile; and they permitted Hemi engines to be run in Belvedere and Coronet bodies on tracks that were shorter than a mile in length.

When the NASCAR tour showed up for the 1965 Firecracker 400, though factory-backed teams were still on the sidelines, Buck and Buddy Baker showed up with Hemi-powered Dodge Polaras (an engine and chassis combination that Householder had said just wouldn't work) and turned in credible performances. As a matter of fact, young Buddy finished the race second to only A.J. Foyt's Banjo Matthews prepped Ford.

It wasn't until July 25 that Chryco and Householder relented and returned to the NASCAR fold under the new rules. Though Richard Petty went on to win four races for Plymouth, and David Pearson three for Dodge, their late season success could not undo the months of inactivity that passed during the boycott. Ford drivers won an incredible 32 consecutive Grand National events in 1965 and all told, fully 48 of the 55 races contested that season. Ned Jarrett was the Grand National champion that year. But, as things turned out, it would be a good long time before a Ford driver visited a NASCAR victory lane again—or won the Grand National championship for that matter!

Return of the Hemi

1966 was the year that Dodge and Plymouth decided to unleash the 426 Hemi on an unsuspecting America. Responding (in part) to Bill France's challenge of 1965 to make the once pure race engine available to the general public, both Dodge and Plymouth car lines offered slightly detuned Hemi engines as regular production options. And both manufacturers wasted little time in letting Bill France know it. On December 13, 1965, France was given a tour of a Hemi engine assembly line. He was favorably impressed and remarked at the time, "I saw more Hemi engines today than Ferrari makes cars in a year." With that stamp of approval, the Hemi engine was made welcome at NASCAR tracks all across the country. As in the last part of the 1965 season, the 426 Hemi was allowed to compete in intermediate (Belvedere and Coronet) chassis on short and intermediate tracks at 426ci. New for 1966 was the option to run those same body styles with destroked, 405ci Hemi on superspeedways, too. As in 1965, full-sized Polaras and Furys could mount a full-sized 426 Hemi for superspeedway work without the need for destroking.

France was no doubt hoping that the new regular production status of the 426 Hemi engine would lead to a peaceful (read: profitable) season on the Grand National tour. But those hopes turned out to be very short lived. In fact, the very same day that France strode down the Hemi assembly line, Ford announced that it intended to campaign its 427ci overhead camshaft Hemi engine during the 1966 NASCAR season. The fact that Ford officials had chosen to make that declaration without notice to the sanctioning body no doubt made France more than a little agitated. His response was brief and to the point and delivered just four days after Ford's precipitous press release: The SOHC 427 engine would not be permitted to race.

Relations between France and Ford quickly became contentious. The first outburst of the coming battle of wills came just before the Christmas holidays when Ford executive, Leo Beebe, announced that Ford would not be able to field cars at either Riverside or Daytona since corporate competition plans for 1966 all revolved around use of the Cammer 427. High level negotiations between France and Ford produced some

concessions, and on Christmas Day, Big Bill announced that the Cammer would be viewed as an experimental engine (due to its non-regular production status) for 1966 and reviewed for competition in 1967. Ford, for its part, announced that it would continue to support stock car racing without interruption. Unfortunately for France, that seeming accord was undone by the superior performance turned in by Hemi teams at the 1966 Daytona 500.

Richard Petty shouted the Hemi's legal arrival at Daytona in 1966 with a hot lap around the 2.5-mile circuit of 175.163 miles per hour in a 405ci powered Belvedere. The twin qualifiers that preceded the 500 were an all-Hemi affair too, with Paul Goldsmith's Plymouth taking one race and Earl Baumer's sleek new "flatback" Charger the other. When the green flag fell on race day, Petty and Goldsmith traded the lead among

Richard Petty used a 426 Hemi engine to bludgeon the competition in 1964 at Daytona where he won just about everything in sight, including the 500 itself. Here the as-yet uncrowned "King" leads Paul Goldsmith, Marvin Panch, Dan Gurney, Darel Dieringer and Sal Toyella through turn four at the Big D. Author collection

Things were quite different for Pearson and his Cotton Owens Dodge in 1966. NASCAR legalized the Hemi again and Ford drivers conducted their own boycott of the series. As a result, Pearson's new flat back Charger was the car to beat for 1966. Not many drivers did, as things turned out. Daytona Speedway Archives

themselves for the first 30 odd laps, and by the end of the event, Hemi-powered cars had led all but 40 laps of the race. It was a humiliating defeat for Ford and one that folks in Dearborn decided to not take sitting down.

Five days after the Daytona 500, Ford announced that the 427 SOHC motor was now a regular production option. Confronted with that assertion from Ford's highest executives, France looked to the Automobile Competition Committee of the United States (ACCUS) (a body that France, incidentally, had no small amount of sway with) for an out. On April 6th ACCUS announced its approval of the 427 SOHC for stock car competition with one significant caveat: Cammer equipped race cars would have to compete with a handicap of nearly 500 pounds.

France and NASCAR adopted that ruling and announced that Cammer 427 would be eligible to compete in 119-inch wheelbase cars (read: the Galaxie line with the specified handicap). As a sop to Ford's tender sensibilities, the sanctioning body also simultaneously announced that two four-barrels would be legal for use on all wedge-headed Ford racing engines. The Chrysler Hemi was limited to one four-barrel carb, but was legalized for use in 116-inch and 119-inch wheelbase cars on all tracks without the need for downsizing.

Unfortunately for France, Ford executives didn't find the new rules provisions to their liking. Ford immediately announced that it was pulling its teams out of three short track races that were next on the schedule. A few days later on Friday, April 15, Ford chief Henry Ford II announced that it was the beginning of a boycott of all NASCAR races. "We can't be competitive under these new rules," Ford said. "We are giving away too much to the Chryslers. And besides that, the safety factor in this is quite important. We couldn't keep wheels on the car at this weight." For the second season in a row, the Grand National stock car series became essentially a one manufacturer show—only this time it was Mopar drivers' turn to have things their own way on the high banks.

Jim Hurtubise (in a Norm Nelson Dodge) and David Pearson had already won an event at Atlanta and Hickory before the Fomoco walkout. Once Ford drivers were safely on the sidelines, Hemi car drivers won the next eight races in a row. In that number were high profile super-speedway triumphs at Darlington in the Rebel 400 (Richard Petty), and at Charlotte in the World 600 (scored by former Ford driver Marvin Panch in a Petty Plymouth).

As in 1965, track owners were more than a little unhappy with the string of single marque wins, and soon Bill France was receiving pressure to modify his stance. France was so desperate to have Ford and Chevrolet drivers in the starting line-up that he had his tech inspectors look the other way when car owners like Smokey Yunick and Junior Johnson took more than a few liberties with the rules book. That willful blindness eventually led to Smokey's allegedly 15/16 scale Chevelle and Johnson's Yellow Banana Galaxie. Though both of those radically rebodied race cars have become legends, their NASCAR permitted deviations away from "stock" still weren't enough to slow the Hemi movement of stock car wins.

Ultimately, Ford drivers returned to the series late in the 1966 season after NASCAR officials modified the rules book to permit Fomoco teams to run intermediate Fairlane and Comet cars that had been fitted with front chassis members borrowed from the 1965/1966 Galaxie line. Interestingly, that rules change was probably the first step towards the totally fabricated chassis that compete on the NASCAR tour today. Though Ford drivers still weren't allowed to run the SOHC 427 engine (which never ran a competitive lap in the NASCAR ranks as things turned out), their downsized intermediate race cars were more of a match for the Hemi-powered Plymouths and Dodges than the block Galaxies they had fielded at the beginning of the season. Darel Dieringer proved that point in spades when he drove a 427-wedge powered Comet to victory in the 1966 Southern 500.

While Fomoco drivers were able to score a few late season wins once they returned to the fray, by the time the rubber dust had settled after the last race of the year, Plymouth and Dodge drivers had won fully 34 of the 49 events contested in 1966. Dodge driver David Pearson came out on top in the seasonal points chase to win his first Grand National driving championship. The 15 wins and 26 top five finishes he turned in that year with his #6 Cotton Owens Dodge earned him $78,193.60 in purse money.

A King Is Crowned; The 1967 Season

When the year 1967 rolled around, it is fair to say that all in the Grand National garage area were hoping for a controversy-free season of NASCAR races. The two boycott years that led up to the 1967 season had been damaging for both the sport and the teams involved in it. All of the top teams and drivers were on hand for Daytona speedweeks 1967 and, at first, harmony prevailed. Mopar drivers were back in force with 426 Hemi-powered Plymouth Belvederes and Dodge Chargers. The cars were just as fast as before. Truth be known, the flat back Chargers were probably even better than before, since NASCAR had allowed Dodge teams to add a rear deck spoiler to aid aerodynamics (a first in the NASCAR ranks). Ford drivers were fast too, especially since the 1967 NASCAR rules book allowed them the use of two four-barrel carburetors and a set of decidedly non-production "Tunnel Port" cylinder heads. Though those castings carried a conventional wedge-shaped combustion chamber, they had been cast up with relocated intake ports so huge that special sealed tubes were needed to run push rods right through the middle of each intake runner (hence the name "Tunnel Port").

Curtis Turner was fastest during qualifying in his more or less "legal" Smokey Yunick prepped Chevelle. The race itself was primarily a battle between Tunnel Port- and Hemi-powered drivers, though, and both LeeRoy Yarbrough's Charger and Fred Lorenzen's Fairlane were fast. USAC star Mario Andretti turned out to be the fastest of all, however. At race's end it was his Tunnel Port-powered Holman & Moody prepped Fairlane that was parked in victory lane. And that fact made Mopar executives more than a little unhappy. Bob Roger was a particularly vocal critic of the non-production heads that had helped power Andretti's Ford to victory. Soon Chrysler executives were making noises about staging another boycott unless the new Ford heads were ruled illegal by the sanctioning body. When NASCAR stood fast behind its ruling that the heads were legal, Chrysler executives sent out the word to their team that they'd appreciate it if those teams would not run the March race in Atlanta as a protest. Unfortunately, there was much less unity among Plymouth and

Dodge drivers in 1967. Richard Petty said publicly that "We (Petty Engineering) race for a living. If they are having a race at Atlanta, we'll be there. In fact, we'll take two cars. If we get a notion, we'll take three cars." That statement pretty much spoke for the rest of the Hemi teams on the tour, too. And so, the threatened Chryco boycott of

Cotton Owens is one of the Grand National (now Winston Cup) series' legendary mechanics. He had a special touch with the 426 Hemi engine and the drivers who campaigned his #6 Dodges won many races as a direct result. Daytona Speedway Archives

1967 died aborning. As things turned out, Ford's new Tunnel Port heads proved to be no match for Chrysler's Hemi engine anyway.

Though Andretti had snared the Daytona 500 win for Ford, the next handful of races fell to Plymouth and Dodge drivers without much effort being expended. Cale Yarborough interrupted that string with a Tunnel Port Fairlane win at Atlanta, but Hemi drivers returned to dominance after the Atlanta 500 and won 20 of the next 25 events contested. Petty Engineering was the big winner in that string as both Richard Petty and team driver Jim Paschal turned in multiple wins. New factory driver Bobby Allison also added to that string of Hemi wins in a Cotton Owens prepped Charger.

In August, Richard Petty went on a tear that's likely to never be duplicated again. Starting with the Meyer Brothers Memorial on the 12th, Petty won the next ten consecutive races. In that number was the 1967 Southern 500 that he won handily, more than five laps ahead of new Holman & Moody driver David Pearson.

Petty's string of wins was broken by Buddy Baker in the National 500 at Charlotte, where Baker whipped the field in a Ray Fox built Hemi Charger. At season's end, Petty had won an incredible 27 events (of 48 starts) and scored 11 other top five finishes. Factoring in Jim Paschal's four wins for Petty Engineering brought that team's total to a stunning 31 for 48 total. Petty's performance won him both a second Grand National driving crown and the now familiar title as the "King of Stock Car Racing." Interestingly, when recently asked the secret of his phenomenal 1967 success, Petty was unable to put his finger on a reason besides lots of luck. Petty went on to say "We were running the same car we had in 1966. Had the same people working on it, same motors. Everything was just naturally a little better. We had another year of experience and we just had phenomenal luck. You run ten races in a row—and finish every lap for ten races in a row—it was quite a season, let alone win the cotton pickin' things. We weren't doing anything different. It was just one of those things." One of those things indeed.

As in 1966, the Hemi Plymouths that Petty drove to glory had all started out as regular production "Bodies in White" Belvederes that had been "bucked" on a UAW assembly line. After arrival in Randleman, North Carolina, the Petty Enterprises crew reinforced the chassis and added a four sidebar roll cage. Race strength torsion bars and "A" frames were added at the bow. A kidney pummeling set of parallel leaf springs and a corporate live axle fitted with floating hubs were mounted aft. Dual shocks were employed to govern each wheel's movement and 3x11-inch fully metallic drum brakes were mounted to scrub off speed. A single four-barrel Hemi was nestled under the Belvedere's stock front sheetmetal and it transferred power to the pavement through a corporate four-speed and a set of track specific gears. Petty kept rein over that 600+ horsepower drivetrain from a production bucket seat perch and with the help of the stock steering wheel and a Hurst Shifter. The car's final cosmetic silhouette was little changed from its assembly line configuration. In fact, save for the slightly flared wheelwells and the 1 1/2-inch rear deck spoiler that the rules book had started allowing in 1967, the car's sheetmetal was pretty much stock. Boxy stock, in fact. And the same was true for the Dodge Chargers that campaigned alongside Petty's #43 Plymouth during the 1967 season. It was just that boxiness that proved to be the two Chryco intermediates' undoing during the 1968 Grand National season.

1968 First Shots of the Aerowars Fired . . . Pictures at Eleven

If Dodge and Plymouth drivers had planned on reprising their "win everything in sight" roles for the 1968 season, they were quickly disabused of that notion during speedweeks at Daytona that year. Though nothing had happened during the off-season to stifle the high horsepower bellow of their 426 Hemi racing engines, there had been a significant change that would greatly affect the on-track fortunes of Plymouth and Dodge drivers during the 49 race 1968 series. That change was improved aerodynamics. Specifically, the greatly improved aerodynamics of the new for 1968 Ford Fairlane and Mercury Montego car lines. Whereas the 1967 iterations of both those intermediate body styles had been squat, sawed off and boxy in configuration, the new model year produced stretched out sleek bodies that featured an exaggerated fastback roofline which flowed unbroken from "A" pillars to the tip of the rear deck lid. Though the 1968 rules book still limited those cars to the same 427 Tunnel Port motors that had been used the season before, their greatly improved aerodynamics promised improved performance without the necessity of improved power production.

Dodge and Plymouth stylists had also been hard at work during the off-season and both the Satellite and Charger lines featured rounded and smoothed body panels that were easier on both the eye and the air than their 1967 counterparts had been. The new for 1968 Dodge Charger line was the most radically changed and seemed to be a sure bet for superspeedway wins. The car's new nose swept from the windshield forward to a slit-like grille that was surrounded by gently curving sheetmetal. The roofline at first glance was swoopy too and seemed to flow smoothly into the deck lid. Unfortunately, the car was not a true fastback as the "flying buttress" "C" pillars that were part of the design actually surrounded a fairly vertical back light. The sleek new nose also had some problems, since it featured a recessed grille sure to catch the superspeedway air just like an open parachute would.

Richard Petty earned the title "King of Stock Car Racing" in 1967 with the help of this Hemi-powered GTX. Petty dominated the series that season winning a grand total of 27 events along with the Grand National championship. Daytona Speedway Archives

Things were even bleaker aerodynamically for Plymouth drivers in 1968. Though their new Road Runners were rounded all over, they carried billboard upright grilles and a sedan style roofline that did not promise to be very efficient at air management.

Still and all, both Mopar chassis carried the potent and by now race-proven 426 Hemi engine. And that was certainly a force that Fomoco drivers had to reckon with. Or, at least, that's what Mopar drivers hoped.

South Carolina driver Cale Yarborough began giving Dodge and Plymouth drivers fits during qualifying for the Daytona 500 when he piloted his Wood brothers Mercury around the track at an average speed of 189.222 miles per hour. Though still relying on one of "last year's" 427 Tunnel Port engines for power, the sleek new sheetmetal that surrounded that #21 car had allowed Yarborough to up the qualifying ante at Daytona by nearly nine miles per hour.

Richard Petty clawed his way to the second

starting spot with a curiously vinyl top equipped Road Runner, but the rest of the top ten qualifiers were pretty much all of the Fomoco persuasion.

That's about how things stayed when the race got under way beneath overcast skies. It wasn't until lap 35 that Buddy Baker's Ray Fox Dodge made it to the front of the pack to lead a lap for Mopar, and that visit was only for one more circuit. Baker ultimately led but one more lap, and his three lap stint out in front, coupled with the one lap lead that Al Unser had posted in Cotton Owens Dodge, represented the only trips around the track led by anything other than a Ford or Mercury. Cale Yarborough's #21 Mercury and LeeRoy Yarbrough's #26 Cyclone spent the most time up front. Cale ultimately led his similarly named but unrelated Mercury rival across the stripe by a bare 1-second margin at the end of the 200 laps that made up the event. It was a humbling defeat for Dodge and Plymouth drivers.

Unfortunately, Mopar drivers didn't fare much better for the balance of the season. Ford and Mercury teams took the next three races after Daytona, and it wasn't until Richard Petty won a 100 miler at Hickory on April 7 that a Mopar car got to visit victory lane. Though NASCAR officials tried to even things out by permitting Mopar teams to run two four-barrel carbs at and after the Rebel 400, Ford and Mercury drivers went on to win 27 of the 49 races run in 1968 including the Rebel 400, the Atlanta 500, Carolina 500, Firecracker 400, Dixie 500 and Southern 500 events.

Buddy Baker did break the Fomoco flow with a big win in the World 600 (in a Ray Fox Charger). Chargin' Charlie Glotzbach made it a Dodge sweep of Charlotte Motor Speedway when he won the National 500 in a Cotton Owens Charger later in the year. And King Richard turned in one superspeedway win at Rockingham in the American 500 in October. But save for those three mile-or-more wins, 1968 was pretty much a blow-out for Fomoco's "Going Thing" and that was all due to aerodynamics.

CHAPTER THREE

1968: THE AEROWARS BEGIN IN EARNEST

As you might have guessed, Chryco executives were none too happy with the result of the 1969 NASCAR season. In just one short season, Plymouth and Dodge drivers had gone from winning almost every race on the tour to being nearly shut out at every superspeedway (and the sports pages that reported race results on Monday morning). It was, to say the least, an intolerable situation. And one that would have to change immediately.

As mentioned, the problem with the Charger's aerodynamics was twofold. The recessed grille that street Chargers carried trapped so much air at racing speeds that it created hundreds of pounds worth of lift. Since lift at the bow of the race car translates into understeer, Dodge drivers had a very hard time getting their cars to turn without backing out of the throttle. Not a good situation when your Fomoco rivals are able to negotiate the same corners with their throttle pedals flat on the floor.

Imagine this in your rearview mirror and you'll understand how intimidating a Dodge Daytona was for Ford and Mercury drivers in 1969. Dodge Daytonas look fast even when they're standing still.

The new Charger's back light caused more than a little consternation, too. Though the car's roofline appeared to be of a fastback design, the "C" pillars were actually hollowed-out to accommodate a nearly vertical back light. Air flowing over the roof at speed tended to become roiled over the hollowed out window recess and that created lift. Not nearly as much of that destabilizing force as the grille did, but more than was optimal for racing purposes.

With the Charger's aerodynamic peccadillos identified, Chrysler engineers set out upon a crash course to correct them in time for the 1969 season. Work got under way with a sketch that had been drawn by engineer John Pointer. The new design featured a grille insert that had been moved forward to a position flush with the front body work and then sealed to it to prevent the admission of any unwanted air. The Charger's rear lift problem was solved by fitting a sheetmetal plug over the hollowed-out "C" pillar area of the roofline. The new plug carried a smaller and flush-fitted back light and created a true fastback roofline. Engineers in Chryco's Special Vehicle Group quickly reproduced Pointer's sketch in clay and soon were testing a 3/8th scale replica of the proposed design in the wind tunnel at Wichita

When the new for 1968 Charger line proved to be aerodynamically challenged, Chryco engineers went back to the drawing board. The end result was the Charger 500. It was the first special body car purpose-built for use on the NASCAR tour. All told, just 392 street-going homologation versions of the 500 were built. That low production number marks cars like the one pictured here (which belongs to Central Florida's Dan Andrews) as some of the rarest built during the musclecar era.

State University. When those wild tunnel tests produced positive results, Dodge executives gave the green light for the production of the 500 street-going "homologation" versions that the NASCAR rules required for any special body style intended for use on the tour. Dodge's answer to the sleek new Fairlanes and Montego line was dubbed the Charger 500. It represented the first time that an American auto manufacturer had created an entirely new car line solely to compete in a form of factory-backed motorsports.

Street-going versions of the new 500 rolled off of the assembly line powered by either 440 wedge-headed single four barrel engines or 426 Hemi big blocks. A number of exterior color combinations were available as were a variety of interior appointments. In every instance, homologation Charger 500s carried the special grille and backlight treatment that had first been suggested by John Pointer's inspired sketch.

Bob Roger's Special Vehicles engineers were convinced they'd created a winner in the new

While street Charger 500s came with both 440 wedge and 426 Hemi engines for power, their racing counterparts relied exclusively on Hemi engines for motorvation.

Charger 500 variant and wasted little time in telling the world so. A press car was made available to motoring scribes at the Chrysler proving grounds as early as June of 1968 and a PR Charger 500 was on hand at Charlotte Motor Speedway for the National 500 in October. In addition to the favorable coverage those early outings received, the new aero-variant's fortunes were also given a boost by the sanctioning body's less than rigorous adherence to its own 500 unit minimum production requirement. Though the Dodge brass had promised that at least 500 street 500s would be built, records available today suggest that no more than 392 of the new NASCAR specials ever rolled off of the assembly line. Then, as now, the NASCAR rules book could become only an "advisory" document when the "good of racing" was involved.

While Dodge drivers had every reason to expect great things from the 1969 Grand National season, their Plymouth stablemates took little cheer in the coming of the new season. That's because their lot that year was to race the same old boxy body styles they'd campaigned the year before. Richard Petty was particularly peeved about that fact and began politicking for a Petty

When the NASCAR circus rolled into Daytona for Speedweeks 1969, there was a flock of aerodynamic Charger 500s in the procession. Bobby Allison's #22 Mario Rossi prepped Charger was in that number. Author collection

Blue Charger 500 to campaign in 1969. Unfortunately for Petty (and ultimately for Plymouth fans everywhere), the Chryco executives he talked to were more than a little short-sighted—and perhaps just a wee bit too confident of both themselves and Petty's Chryco allegiance. As it happens, Ford's racing tsar, Jacque Passino, had been courting Petty for some time. His plan was to make Petty a card-carrying member of Ford's Going Thing. When Petty's request for a new Charger 500 was summarily denied, he picked up the phone and dialed Passino's Dearborn number. A short time later, he signed a one-year contract as a Ford driver.

But it wasn't just money that persuaded Petty to jump ship and throw in his lot with Ford. In point of fact, it was aerodynamics. What Dodge drivers didn't know as they looked eagerly towards the 1969 season is that they wouldn't be the only drivers campaigning an all-new aero-variant during the next year.

Unbeknownst to them and the rest of the racing world, Ralph Moody and Ford stylist Larry Shinoda had been hard at work on a slicked-up version of the Fairlane fastback body. Moody's task was made easier by the fact that the Fairlane (and Montego) car line did not suffer from the same unwanted lift problems over the rear window that the standard Charger body did. So Moody concentrated his efforts solely on cleaning up the Fairlane's front end. Part of the program cooked up by Moody in the super secret back room at Holman & Moody's Charlotte complex was moving the Fairlane's normally recessed grille approximately six inches ahead of stock. Next, Moody grafted on a set of sheetmetal stampings that both narrowed and tapered the car's profile on their way towards mating with the moved-up grille. A special header panel was used to connect Moody's newly extended fenders just ahead of the stock hood. A new front bumper cut and welded to form a rudimentary air foil rounded out the new variant's design. Ford executives called the new car the Torino Talladega, after Bill France's then under construction superspeedway in Alabama. When wind tunnel tests provided positive results, Ford boss Bunkie Knudsen gave the green light for Talladega homologation. All told, 754 street Talladegas were built in time to satisfy NASCAR's production requirements. When Ford teams began rolling into the garage area for Daytona speedweeks 1969 they came packing long-nosed Talladegas. In that number was one particular Petty blue car that carried familiar #43 markings.

Pre-race preparations for the 500 got under way on a high note for Dodge drivers. That's because superspeedway specialist Buddy Baker drew first aerodynamic blood for Charger 500 drivers by snatching up the pole with a 188.901 miles per hour hot lap. David Pearson took some of the edge off of that triumph, when he tripped the clocks at 190.029 just a few days later, to become the fastest qualifier for the race. Pearson

When Charger 500s fell short of the mark, Dodge engineers returned to the drawing board in search of aerosuperiority. Their answer was to graft on a radical new beak and soaring rear deck spoiler to the basic 500 package. The end result was the Charger Daytona. Chargin' Charlie Glotzbach drove winged Daytonas for Ray Nichels during the aerowars. Glotzbach was a notorious lead-foot and he wasted little time tapping into the new aerocar's potential. During testing at the Chrysler proving grounds, for example, Glotzbach quickly had his winged car running in the 240 mile per hour range. Author collection

backed up that performance with a solid win in the first of the two traditional pre-500 qualifiers. Bobby Isaac scored the first Charger 500 (and ultimately only) superspeedway win just a few hours later when his K&K Insurance Charger 500 crossed the stripe first in the second qualifier.

Buddy Baker translated his pole starting berth into the lead for the first three laps of the 500 itself. Cale Yarborough claimed the top spot for Ford on lap four and Talladega drivers went on to lead 118 of the race's 200 laps including the all-important final one. LeeRoy Yarbrough's Big T was first across the line and finished one car length ahead of Charlie Glotzbach's day-glo #6 Charger 500.

To say that Dodge drivers were disappointed by the results of the much-anticipated Daytona 500 is an understatement. Special Vehicle's engineer, Larry Rathgeb, was forced to admit that the Talladega "was superior in aerodynamics and in performance to the Charger 500." His colleague George Wallace added that "Overall,

Bobby Allison ranks as one of the greatest drivers in NASCAR history. In 1969 and 1970, he campaigned a flashy Dodge Daytona for Mario Rossi. With Allison at the helm, that car was powered by a full race 426ci Hemi engine. In 1971, Dick Brooks drove the same car in the Daytona 500 under the power of a 305ci small block engine. That race turned out to be the last event on the Grand National tour for a Chrysler winged car. Author collection

Dodge teams weren't any better off than they had been the season before." Fortunately, though Chrysler engineers like Rathgeb and Wallace were dejected after Daytona, they were far from being defeated. And that was a good thing, since Mopar racing fortunes were destined to get a whole lot worse that year before they improved. David Pearson snapped up wins at the next two short track races on the 1969 tour before Bobby Allison was able to win a trophy for Dodge at Bristol in the Southwestern 500. Joy from that short track win was short-

lived for the "Dodge Boys" however, because Fomoco teams showed up one week later packing a new double whammy at Atlanta.

Ford's desire to field a Hemi-headed race engine of its own was well known. It was at Atlanta in 1969 that Fomoco realized that goal, when the sanctioning body finally allowed the all-new Boss 429 Hemi to compete. Ford teams had actually arrived at Daytona with Boss '9s parked under the hoods of their long-nosed Talladegas, but when Bill France balked at the engine's homologation status (France asserted that the necessary 500 street-going Boss 429 Mustangs hadn't been built), Ford teams were forced to yank the new motors and replace them with tried and true 427 Tunnel Port wedges. France lifted his Boss '9 ban just before the Atlanta race, the second superspeedway event of note on the 1969 schedule. As if things weren't bad enough for Dodge and Plymouth drivers at that race, the Atlanta 500 was also the race that Mercury drivers got an aero-variant of their own to campaign. The car was called the Cyclone Spoiler II, and like its Talladega counterparts, the new Merc sported a stretched and drooped nose. Worse yet for Mopar drivers, the new Spoiler II's body work was actually one to two miles per hour faster than the Talladega.

Cale Yarborough drove that point home (literally) by handily winning the Atlanta 500 in his first outing in a Boss '9 powered Spoiler II. The balance of the 1969 season was characterized by a string of Charger 500 victories on short tracks (where the 426 Hemi seemed to produce more low end grunt than the new Ford motor) bracketed by a string of mile-or-more superspeedway wins all captured by the aerodynamically superior Talladega Fords and Spoiler II Mercurys. Fomoco wins at high-profile headline-generating races like the Rebel 400, the World 600, the Motor State 500, the Firecracker 400, the Dixie 500, the Yankee 600 and the Southern 500 served to cause Special Vehicles engineers to redouble their efforts to overcome the Fomoco aero advantage. Their solution was both innovative and radical. The end result was a pair of purpose built stock car racing intermediates that set the racing world on its ear.

The Wing's the Thing

Shortly after the debacle in Daytona, Dodge engineers had returned to the drawing board in search of even better aerodynamic performance. As with the Charger 500 project, early work on Dodge's answer to the Torino Talladega came straight from the pen of John Pointer. Working

Racing exploits of Dodge Daytona drivers were made possible by a homologation run of street-going cars like this one. Like their racer counterparts, those street cars all carried pointy beaks and soaring rear wings. The rear spoiler on a Dodge Daytona consisted of three elements: a horizontal cross bar shaped like an inverted airplane wing and two tear drop-shaped upright struts. Working in concert those alloy components created both down force and stability.

closely with Bob Marcell, Pointer cooked up an all-new version of the Charger body which sported a pointy beak and radical rear wing that soared several feet above the rear deck lid. The essential purpose of those added appendages was, of course, to further smooth the flow of air at racing speeds.

Dodge product planner Dale Reeker and Special Vehicle engineer Larry Rathgeb were enthusiastic about the sketches and passed them on to higher-ups for production approval. That final okay came from Dodge Veep and GM Bob McCurry. After scanning the artwork that Rathgeb and Reeker had presented, McCurry simply asked

Next
The nose on a Charger Daytona was designed to slice through the air like a hot knife through butter. Formed out of sheetmetal, the radical new beak created nearly 200 pounds of positive down force over the front wheels of a race car at superspeedway velocities.

Dodge Daytonas and Plymouth Superbirds represented the last word in both aerodynamics and factory commitment to motorsports competition. It's unlikely that we'll ever see the likes of them again.

if the new car would win races. An answer in the affirmative was quickly forthcoming. So, too, was McCurry's corporate blessing. The only fly in the ointment for the new project was the necessity of having the new car in ready-to-race trim by September 1969—the scheduled date of the very first Grand National stock car race at Alabama International Speedway (aka Talladega). The new track's inaugural race was sure to capture a lot of media attention and Dodge executives wanted to capitalize on that gathering of scribes by debuting the new stock car at the same time. That deadline left an impossibly short seven months to turn Pointer and Marcell's sketches into functional sheetmetal let alone to build the 500 homologation cars needed to satisfy the sanctioning body. So the race was on for Special Vehicles engineers.

The starting point for the project was a 1968 Charger chassis that had been built for use by Charlie Glotzbach in the Firecracker 400. That particular chassis just happened to be on hand since it had originally been built to bend the rules book a

bit via non-stock lowering (two inches both front and rear). When NASCAR tech inspectors caught on to the car's "cheated up" configuration, its active racing days were over. First work on the as-yet-unnamed car's new beak began in late January. Two different versions of Pointer's original design were mocked up in 3/8ths scale first and then wind tunnel tested back at Wichita State. That test data was then translated into a full-sized clay nose that had been grafted onto the snout of Glotzbach's old Charger for further testing in the Lockheed aircraft wind tunnel in Georgia.

While one team of engineers was busy working on the aero-variant's beak, yet another group was endeavoring to recreate Pointer's soaring rear wing in sheetmetal. Differing wing heights and configurations were tested. With time and testing it was decided to make the wing's horizontal cross member an inverted airfoil that was designed to produce positive downforce. Dodge aerodynamicist Gary Romberg played a large role in final wing configuration and his work ultimately led to shaping of the wing's uprights as airfoils, too. The final decision was just how far to position the horizontal wing section above the car's rear deck. Test heights of 6, 12 and 15 inches were tried. Ultimately, an elevation of 23 inches was settled on for no other reason than that height allowed the abbreviated trunk lid to open fully—an important consideration when you factor in the rules mandated fleet of street-going cars that would have to be built.

As with the design changes charted up for the new design's nose, Romberg's rear wing prototypes were first tested in 3/8ths scale and then transferred to the Glotzbach car for full-size wind tunnel work. In addition to the new wing and nose work, the aero-variant was ultimately fitted with two rear-facing air scoops that mounted atop the front fenders directly over the tires. Though swoopy looking and seemingly aerodynamic in nature, in truth, the new scoops were last-minute add-ons designed to provide more tire clearance when the suspension was fully compressed at racing speeds.

And in a way, suspension compression was just what the new race car was all about. Wind tunnel testing of the new beak and bustle showed that when those components were bolted onto the basic Charger 500 unit body, 200 tire shredding pounds of positive downforce were produced over the front wheels and 600+ (depending on wing angle) at the rear. Actual track testing

with a race spec car left Dodge drivers like Buddy Baker and Glotzbach smiling from ear to ear and boasting that they could navigate Daytona with just one hand on the steering wheel.

Dodge executives opted to name the new car after that very track, Bill France's Daytona International Speedway. The wraps were pulled off of the new Daytona in April of 1969 when the motoring press was treated to a mockup that had been hastily cobbled from fiberglass components and a Charger 500 chassis. A photo op with a race car

Bobby Isaac drove winged Daytonas for Harry Hyde and the K&K insurance team in 1969 and 1970. Isaac was one of the only factory team drivers to stick around for the boycotted inaugural Talladega 500. One of Isaac's cars is currently on display at the International Motorsports Hall of Fame in Talladega today.

Buddy Baker drove a Daytona for Cotton Owens during the aerowars. He won the Southern 500 in 1970 in a day-glo #6 car just like this one. This particular Daytona is on display at the Joe Weatherly Museum in Darlington. Mike Slade

mockup sporting an early version of the rear wing was also arranged for the press at the Chrysler proving grounds in Chelsea, Michigan.

The Charger Daytona's debut left motoring scribes in a hyperbolic frenzy—just the result that Dodge PR types were hoping for. Yet while the new radically winged car looked fast during photo ops, the question as to its actual race track performance remained unanswered. Side-by-side top speed tests were conducted with a race spec Daytona and an equally racey Charger 500 at Chelsea in July of 1969. Those results were mixed. The performance goal set for the new Daytona during development was a five mile per hour increase in top speed without the introduction of additional horsepower (as a rule of thumb, it takes about 15 extra horsepower to generate each additional

Cotton Owens was a master at setting up a race Hemi engine. In peak tune, Owens was able to coax in excess of 650 ponies out of an engine like this one. When coupled with the Dodge Daytona's aero-package, that grunt translated into near double ton super-speedway velocities.

mile per hour of top speed at tracks like Daytona and Talladega). While the new Daytona proved to be faster than the old 500, it was only just. But within a week of taking it to the track, Dodge drivers and engineers had pumped up the top speed to an impressive 205 miles per hour average around the five-mile Chrysler banked track. By the time Chelsea testing was completed, Glotzbach had pushed the envelope out to an incredible 243 miles per hour. Soon all involved with the project were looking forward to September and Talladega with undisguised glee.

Charger Daytona teams began arriving in Talladega, Alabama, during the third week of August 1969. They had no idea what to expect of the new track because it had been built as the longest (2.66 mile) and steepest (banking at Talladega is 33 degrees) on the Grand National tour. But they were anxious to find out how their new winged car would perform on a real race track under drafting conditions.

Their first few laps around the track were an unsettling experience. As it turned out, the track surface was both green and very rough. Ripples in the corners caused drivers to bounce up and down about three inches in cycles of 40 seconds or so. That had to be an unnerving experience for a driver who was hurtling around the track at more than 190 miles per hour and under the influence of more than 2Gs (times the weight of normal gravity).

When Ford teams arrived, their drivers began to complain of the same high speed oscillations that the Daytonas had experienced. As Chryco and Fomoco testing continued, a new and even more ominous problem reared its ugly head: tire blistering. Though both Goodyear and Firestone had been hard at work on a tire that was up to the task of taming Talladega, their best efforts had fallen short of the mark. Sustained high speed running quickly caused blistering on the treaded tires of the day, which if left unchecked, resulted in potentially catastrophic

Like all race spec Daytonas, the control cabin in Baker's #6 car was purposefully spartan. A single production-based bucket seat kept Buddy behind the tape-wrapped wheel and within easy reach of the Hurst floor shifter. Note the engine electronics package that was mounted in the passenger's floor well.

high speed blow-outs. While testing continued, both tire companies burned the midnight oil in search of a compound and configuration that would take the gaff. Treadless stock car tires were even tried for the very first time on the NASCAR circuit. But nothing seemed to work.

Though drivers in both of the aero-warring camps were concerned about track conditions, testing and qualifying continued unabated and track speeds began to climb as teams came closer to sorting their cars out. Charlie Glotzbach was consistently fast in both his own #99 Nichels Engineering Daytona and during test sessions with the Chrysler engineering #88 Mule that was not slated to actually run in the event. Glotzbach's earliest laps topped the 185 mark with ease. On September 9, 1969, Glotzbach took the test mule out for a spin and topped 199 miles per hour (199.987 miles per hour to be

Buddy Baker became the first driver to officially break the 200 mile per hour mark in a stock car in March of 1970. He used this Chryco R&D Daytona to turn in a 200.096 mile per hour lap at Talladega to set that record. Baker's record setter is still at Talladega on display in the International Motorsports Hall of Fame that's located there.

exact). Glotzbach returned to a garage area characterized by equal parts jubilation and consternation. The new all-time record top speed was certainly something to crow about (if you happened to be a Dodge driver, that is) but Glotzbach was also in more than a little hot water since he'd been ordered not to exceed 185 miles per hour due to safety concerns.

When pole qualifying day rolled around, Bobby Isaac turned out to be the fastest driver on the track and his #71 K&K Dodge tripped the lights at an official new NASCAR record speed of 199.386 miles per hour. Though Glotzbach was

trumped on pole day, he still copped fastest qualifier laurels with a lap of 199.466 in his Dow Chemicals Daytona. The scene seemed to be set for a winged car blow-out on race day. But when race day dawned over Talladega, Glotzbach and most of the other top flight drivers were nowhere to be found.

A driver boycott of the event led by Richard Petty and the Professional Driver's Association (PDA) had pretty much emptied out the garage area. When Bill France had been unable to satisfy the drivers' concerns about track conditions (with no quick fixes available, France had been reduced to suggesting that drivers "race" more slowly!), drivers honoring the PDA boycott pulled their cars out of A.I.M.S. on Saturday evening before the scheduled Sunday race. France was forced to crazy quilt a starting field for the featured 500 out of the few remaining Grand National cars in the garage area and a score of the Grand American Mustangs, Camaros and Javelins that had run an "undercard" event and were still at the track. In that number was the #99 car that Glotzbach had used to set the fastest lap. But when the green flag fell it was journeyman driver Richard Brickhouse who flat pedaled the car across the stripe.

Bobby Isaac was one of the few name drivers who had not caravaned out of the track with the PDA, and his #71 Daytona led the field for its first trip around the track. None of the long-nosed Talladegas and Spoiler IIs that the winged Daytonas had been designed to humble were in the field. And even if they had been, any real test of aerodynamic supremacy between the two breeds of factory aero-warriors would have been undone by the great number of mandatory tire check pit stops that France had imposed on the event to prevent high speed shunts from occurring. Brickhouse got to kiss the pretty girl in

Baker's R&D Daytona was powered by a NASCAR spec 426 Hemi. Note the roll cage assembly that extended under the hood of the #88 car and tied into its reinforced, torsion bar chassis.

Chryco built three different aero-cars to do battle with Fomoco and the forces of evil during the 1969 and 1970 seasons—the Charger 500, the Charger Daytona and the Superbird. Whether wearing street plumage or race car war paint, a Chryco winged car is a radical looking beast. Tim Wellborn owns the two low mileage street wings pictured here, while the K&K car is on display at the International Motorsports Hall of Fame in Talladega.

Talladega's victory lane, but when all was said and done, the first Grand National victory scored by a Chrysler winged car was a hollow one indeed.

The first real test of superspeedway superiority came four races later at Charlotte in the National 500. With high speed oscillations and tire blistering problems behind them, Fomoco and Dodge drivers had no excuses for not turning in their best performances on the banked 1.5-mile Charlotte Motor Speedway. Though many in the C.M.S. garage area (including more than a few Fomoco drivers) predicted that the new winged Dodges would sweep all of the top starting positions during qualifying, things didn't turn out as planned. Cale Yarborough proved to be the fastest of all during qualifying and his long-nosed Cyclone Spoiler II set a record-setting speed of 162.162 miles per hour (a speed fully six miles per hour faster than Charlie Glotzbach's pole speed of one year before). Richard Petty's #43 Talladega was just a tick slower and claimed the outside pole. All told, Fomoco drivers claimed the first four starting positions and the closest a Daytona

driver come to the front of the pack was Buddy Baker's fifth place berth. Fastest qualifier Yarborough said of the new winged cars after qualifying, "We (Fomoco drivers) had looked at those cars and wondered quite a bit about how we would stack up. It's a great feeling to win the pole under these circumstances."

While Fomoco drivers were feeling great, Dodge drivers like Baker, Isaac and Glotzbach could only grumble. As things turned out, events during the race did little to improve their mood. When the field was given its head, Donnie Allison charged to the lead in his poppy red Banjo Matthews prepped Talladega and held onto the top slot for 25 laps. Dodge drivers Dave Marcis, Buddy Baker and Bobby Allison led the field in turn for the next 86 circuits before handing the baton back to Fomoco forces. When the white flag was shown to the field, it was Donnie Allison who was out in front again. He not only won the race that day, his #27 Talladega also led the most laps (154 of 334). After the event, Allison said, "Once I went to the front early, I knew I could handle just about anyone if nothing happened." Things had definitely not gone as planned for Dodge drivers in the first legitimate head-to-head test of aerodynamic superiority with Talladega and Spoiler II drivers. After the race, blame for that fact was placed on tire failure and Daytona drivers complained that their winged cars became undriveably loose after just 10 or 15 laps on fresh tires.

The next mile-or-more superspeedway race on the 1969 schedule came at Rockingham in the American 500. Daytona drivers, still licking their wounds from their defeat at Charlotte, hoped for better results at the Rock. Qualifying results provided reason for optimism as Charlie Glotzbach outpaced all comers with a 136.972 miles per

hour circuit of the 1.07-mile superspeedway. Bobby Allison was only a fraction of a second slower in his #22 Mario Rossi prepped Daytona and started the race on the outside pole. LeeRoy Yarbrough's Talladega was the fastest of all, however, and his Talladega turned in a top speed of 137.732 miles per hour during post pole day practice sessions. Though Daytona drivers had hoped to turn in their first superspeedway defeat of the long-nosed Fomoco hoards, it was not to be at Rockingham. At race's end, LeeRoy Yarbrough was awarded his seventh superspeedway trophy of the 1969 season. Talladega teammate David Pearson came home in second in his #17 Big T one lap behind Yarbrough. Buddy Baker's #6 Daytona finished six more laps

Dodge Daytonas were designed with high banked, superspeedway action in mind. Here's a gaggle of those cars in their element at Daytona in 1970. Author collection

Plymouth executives were distraught after Richard Petty jumped ship for Ford in 1969. They resolved to get him back no matter what the cost. The Plymouth Superbird was a direct result of that endeavor. Petty protege Pete Hamilton drove the #40 Superbird for Petty Enterprises in 1970. Author collection

down to the winner to claim third place. Though Baker and his Daytona teammates had spent their first two superspeedway outings getting a good look at the rear bumper of a long-nosed Fomoco product, big track victory was waiting for them just around the corner.

The last race of the season was a 500-mile affair contested on the two-mile superspeedway located just outside College Station, Texas. The Texas 500, though now but a memory from a

race no longer on the circuit, is still a race worthy of remembrance since it was the setting for the first wing car win over Fomoco's long-nosed aero-cars on a superspeedway.

Buddy Baker claimed the pole position for the event with a speed of 176.284 miles per hour. David Pearson's Talladega was only a few hundredths off of that frantic pace, though and started the race alongside Baker's Daytona in the second spot. Baker translated the top starting spot into the lead of the most laps during the race and all told, Baker's day-glo #6 Dodge was out in front dominating 150 of 250 laps contested. In fact, Baker's third Grand National win seemed all but in the bag, until on lap 228 he ran smack dab into the back of James Hylton's Daytona—while the field was running under caution! It seems that Baker had taken his eyes off of the track as he passed pit road in order to flash his crew the victory sign. That victory was lost in the resulting crash. Chryco officials along pit road were visibly upset about Baker's misstep as that shunt at first appeared to end their last chance for a big track winged car win in 1969. Fortunately, when Baker bowed out, Bobby Isaac stepped up to provide that hoped-for win. He wheeled his orange Daytona across the stripe two full laps ahead of second place finisher David Pearson's Talladega.

When the first full season of the factory-backed aerowars was in the books, David Pearson and Fomoco had come out on top. Pearson's 11 wins and 42 top five finishes had secured his second straight (and third total) Grand National championship. Richard Petty's first year in a Ford was also a successful one, and his ten wins placed him second in the points chase. Overall, Ford drivers scored 26 Grand National wins with their Mercury stablemates adding four more for a total of 30 wins. Dodge drivers turned in 22 mostly short track wins, and their Plymouth compatriots recorded two. Things would be very different indeed the following season.

Major changes were taking place behind the scenes at both Chryco and Fomoco well before the end of the 1969 season. The big news at Plymouth was the production of an all-new winged warrior that was based on the Satellite/Road Runner chassis. As already reported, folks in the Mayflower division were more than a little stung by long-time Plymouth partisan Richard Petty's departure for Ford and an aerodynamic Talladega. Shortly after his defection, Plymouth "powers

When Richard Petty lost an engine during the early laps of the 1970 Daytona 500, it seemed that the new Plymouth Superbird's competition debut would be spoiled. Pete Hamilton saved the day by slipping past David Pearson's Talladega during the waning laps of the race to cross the stripe first. Author collection

that be" came to their senses and resolved to move heaven and earth to get the King of stock car racing back behind the wheel of a Road Runner. Since the source of Petty's unhappiness was the lack of a slippery new aero-car built by Plymouth, it was an absolute no brainer for executives in that division to order up a winged car of their own. Covert overtures were made to Petty in June of 1969. When he indicted a willingness to return to the fold if a suitable winged Plymouth was built, the commitment was made to build just such a car that very same month. As with the Daytona project of one-half season before, George Wallace, Gary Romberg, Larry Rathgeb and the Special Vehicles team were given the task of cooking up a winged Road Runner.

Though one might have thought that creating a winged Plymouth would be easy for the

A soaring rear wing was a part of both the Dodge Daytona and the Plymouth Superbird packages. Though slightly different in configuration, a Superbird's wing was just as effective at creating a down force as a Daytona's tail feathers were.

team of engineers who had come up with similar aero-plumage for the Dodge Charger line, it was actually a tougher task than it appeared. First, RPO Satellite fenders were not easily adaptable to the fitting of a Daytona styled nose cone. Second, a Satellite's rear window could not be modified in exactly the same way that a Charger 500/Daytona's back light had been. Finally, whereas race engineers had been pretty much left alone while designing the Dodge Daytona, office politics and rivalry between Special Vehicles engineers and styling studio types was allowed to gum up the works during design work on the new winged Plymouth. Adding to these difficulties was the new NASCAR rule that now required not just 500 homologation cars to be built, but 1,000—or one car for half of the total number of Plymouth dealerships, whichever was greater.

Those problems notwithstanding, work on the new winged car did get under way. One of the first steps in that process was the installation of Dodge Coronet fenders on the front of a Satellite unit body. As it turned out, Dodge fenders were much more suitable for the addition of a pointed Daytona style nose than standard Plymouth sheet metal was. With fenders in place, a new air

A Plymouth Superbird's beak came to a higher point than a Dodge Daytona's did. As a result, a larger front spoiler was needed to help manage the air that confronted the car at superspeedway velocities. Ramo Stott drove this Superbird in both NASCAR and ARCA events in 1970. Miraculously, it survived its racing career in remarkably good shape.

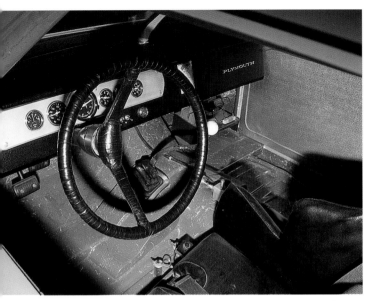

The cockpit of a race spec Superbird was an austere place. It contained little more than a production-based bucket seat and the basic (and non-power assisted) controls necessary to shepherd the car around a racing circuit with expedition. Note the essentially stock dash panel that was still part of the NASCAR program in 1970.

Race Hemis were part of the performance recipe for Plymouth drivers in 1970. This Petty Enterprises prepped mill sports a ram box single 4V intake and cowl induction fed induction system.

scything nose was formed from sheet steel and made to work in unison with the Dodge fender/Plymouth hood front clip.

Work at the rear of the car included the development of an air flow smoothing rear window plug that carried a smaller than stock backlight. A Daytona style three element wing was also part of the program. Interestingly, the wing devised for the new Plymouth was a bit different in size than the airfoil first developed for the Daytona.

As with Daytona R&D work, 3/8ths scale models of proposed designs were wind tunnel tested first, and then translated into full-sized components for further aerodynamic evaluation. By late summer 1969, Special Vehicles engineers were track testing a race car mockup of the new car and final negotiations were under way with Richard Petty regarding his return to Plymouth for

1970. Chryco executives called the new winged wonder the Plymouth Superbird, and scheduled its racing debut for the first race of the 1970 NASCAR season: the Motor Trend 500 at Riverside Raceway in California.

Over at Ford, work was also under way in preparation for the 1970 season during the early days of the 1969 series. Ford and Mercury car lines were scheduled to undergo a complete redesign for the upcoming model year and that necessitated the development of two all-new aero-variants of the Fairlane and Montego models. Famed stylist Larry Shinoda (designer of the split window Corvette, the Z-28 Camaro and the Boss 302 Mustang) was given the task of drawing up the aero-add-ons needed to make the new and larger 1970 Ford and Mercury intermediate bodies into superspeedway winners. The design Shinoda settled on featured a whole new front clip made up of a block-long hood and radically extended fenders that carried fared headlights. The overall look was quite similar to the nose on an early 240 Datsun Z car and the hoodline rose from just above pavement level in a smooth arc that terminated at the wind screen.

Research and development work on the new

aero-design had progressed to the point of naming the new Ford the Torino King Cobra (with the Mercury version referred to as the Super Spoiler II) by the middle of 1969. Fiberglass beaks were fitted to a number of street prototypes and at least one race chassis for evaluation. Early tests were conducted at Daytona with a Holman & Moody prepped car driven by Wood brothers Mercury driver Cale Yarborough. Preliminary results indicated that the new nose worked well. Too well, in fact. It struck the front tires to the tarmac so well that the rear tires lost traction. Ford engineers were hard at work on a new rear window, and

possibly even a Daytona style wing, when the bottom fell out of Ford motorsports funding.

The agent behind that change in Ford racing fortunes was Lee Iacocca. When Ford chief and inveterate racer Semon Bunkie Knudsen got the boot from Henry Ford II late in 1969, he was replaced by Lee Iacocca. Iacocca's vision of Ford's future focused on thrifty (read: boring) little commuter cars like the Pinto and Maverick and did not include factory-backed motorsports competition. One of his first acts as chief executive was to cut Fomoco racing budgets a withering 75 percent across the board. By the end of the 1971

Though pleasing to the eye, the sheetmetal carried by a late sixties Road Runner was not exactly aerodynamically efficient. Plymouth engineers cured those deficiencies with an add-on beak and a radical rear deck wing.

Richard Petty was more than a little unhappy when he was told he'd have to campaign a boxy Plymouth Road Runner for the 1969 season. He was so unhappy, in fact, he jumped ship to run a Ford.

season, Ford was out of the racing business altogether. Iacocca's axe killed the Torino King Cobra project aborning and relegated Ford drivers to last year's Talladegas and Spoiler IIs for 1970. It also hamstrung the production of special racing high-performance parts and suspension components, and put corporate racing factory, Holman & Moody, on a bread-and-water diet. And so it was that Chrysler's record-shattering winged warriors won the second round of the factory-backed aerowars in 1970, well before the first race of that historic season was run.

1970 Winged Cars Take Flight

1970 was destined to be the high water mark of Chryco's factory-backed racing efforts, though few probably realized it at the time. The NASCAR season got under way with a road course race at Riverside that year and a whole new flock of winged Plymouths were on hand to show their tail feathers to the rest of the field. First and foremost in that number was King Richard Petty. Plymouth's all-new Superbird and the promise to make Petty Engineering the "Holman & Moody of the Mopar world" (read: Petty would pick up responsibility for the construction of all future Chryco stock car chassis) had brought the prodigal Plymouth son home. Not to be overlooked was the winged Plymouth fielded by former Ford partisan Dan Gurney's West Coast team. Signing Gurney for Trans-Am and NASCAR duty had been quite a coup for Plymouth executives and his Petty prepped 'Bird received more than a little ink. Gurney got the season off to a promising start with a pole winning lap around the challenging course at 112.060 miles per hour. Though A.J. Foyt went on to win the event in a Jack Bowsher Torino, great

things were waiting for Superbird drivers just down the NASCAR road.

When the NASCAR circus rolled into Daytona for speedweeks 1970 there were no fewer than 18 wing car teams in the van. Cale Yarborough proved that though poorly funded, Fomoco teams were far from defeated by cinching the pole position with a 194.015 qualifying lap. Yarborough turned that top speed potential into a win at the first of the twin qualifiers that precede the 500 each year. Charlie Glotzbach claimed top honors for Daytona drivers in the second Daytona "twin"

The car that persuaded King Richard to join Ford's Going Thing was a long-nosed Torino Talladega. Though Fomoco executives were happy he made the switch, Mopar fans were prostrate with grief. Author collection

While Dodge engineers were hard at work on the Charger 500 in late 1968, their Fomoco rivals were not resting on their laurels. Ralph Moody, Larry Shinoda and a team of Fomoco aerodynamicists pooled their talents to create the Torino Talladega. Though wingless, Talladegas (and their Mercury counterparts, the Cyclone Spoiler II) ultimately won the aerowars by scoring 23 super-speedway victories to Dodge and Plymouth's 13 during the 1969 and 1970 seasons.

to make it Fomoco 1, Mopar 1 heading into the 500 itself.

Yarborough outdistanced outside pole sitter Buddy Baker's Daytona as the pack headed into the first turn of lap one in the 500 and held that lead for the first few circuits. Glotzbach and a series of Daytona drivers took command next, and when King Richard blew an engine on lap seven, it looked as if the 500 would again be a Dodge and Fomoco show. But that's not how things turned out. At 192 laps into the race, new Petty protege, Pete Hamilton, slipped past David Pearson's H&M Talladega to claim the lead for Superbird. For the next seven laps he held off all challenges from Pearson and when the flag fell, a

Superbird had won its first superspeedway event. It was but a hint of the winged car dominance that would characterize the 1970 season.

Richard Petty won the very next superspeedway event on the schedule at Rockingham to make it two for two: Superbird. Bobby Allison beat Cale Yarborough by a mere 50 feet to win the Atlanta 500 in his gold and red #22 Daytona, and

Opposite page
Pete Hamilton's win in the 1970 Daytona 500 (among others) was made possible by the homologation run of street legal Superbirds required by the NASCAR rules book. Street 'Birds today remind Plymouth fans of the days when the factory spared no expense in achieving Grand National glory.

The 1970 Daytona 500 was the first time that all four of the special aero-cars developed by Fomoco and Chryco (the Talladega, the Spoiler II, the Daytona and the Superbird) went head to head in superspeedway trim. Pete Hamilton's #40 Superbird carried the day and won that new winged car's first competitive outing. Author collection

when the tour rolled around to Talladega, it was Pete Hamilton who proved his Daytona win was no fluke by trouncing the field in the first "legitimate" (read: non-boycotted) Grand National contest at A.I.M.S. Bobby Isaac came home second in the Alabama 500, more than a lap ahead of the closest Talladega driver, David Pearson.

Pearson scored the first long track win for Ford in the Rebel 400 at Darlington, and Donnie Allison proved there was still some life left in the beleaguered Fomoco forces by winning the World 600 in a Banjo Matthews prepped Talladega two weeks later. Cale Yarborough won again for Mercury at Michigan in the Motor State 400 on June 7th. Donnie Allison won the Firecracker 400 for Fomoco, too, but after that

Plymouth's intermediate body style was even worse aerodynamically than its Dodge stablemates in 1968. As a result, fastback Ford and Mercury drivers won most of the high profile superspeedway events that year. Richard Petty's boxy Satellite featured a novel vinyl roof in the 1968 Daytona 500. Though rumored to be an aerodynamic secret weapon, it didn't help much during the race. Daytona Speedway Archives

win, the rains came for Ford and Mercury drivers as Daytona and Superbird drivers won the next 19 straight events. In that number were long track wins at Dover, Atlanta and Trenton for Richard Petty; Talladega (again) for Pete Hamilton; and Darlington for Buddy Baker (in the prestigious Southern 500).

LeeRoy Yarbrough rallied for Mercury with a mile-or-more win in the National 500 at Charlotte and Cale Yarborough made it two superspeedway wins in a row for Spoiler IIs with a triumph at Rockingham in the American 500.

When the season ended, Daytona and Superbird drivers had won 38 of 47 races they contested.

Mercury's aerowarrior was the Cyclone Spoiler II. Like the Talladega it featured an extended nose. And like the Talladega it was fast—even without a soaring rear deck wing. All told, Spoiler IIs (like LeeRoy Yarbrough's #98 car) and Talladegas (like Richard Petty's #43 car) won 23 superspeedway events in 1969 and 1970 compared to just 13 for Chryco aero-cars. Author collection

Bobby Isaac came out on top in the season points chase and his 11 wins and 32 top five finishes earned his K&K Daytona team $199,600 and the Grand National title. It had been an incredible season of triumph for Chryco's winged warriors. Unfortunately, it was also to be the last full season for winged cars and their long-nosed Fomoco rivals. Though work was still under way at Chryco's Special Vehicles division on a second generation of aerowarriors, Big Bill France brought a halt to that endeavor when he announced that any special aerobodied car that chose to compete on the Grand National series in 1971 would be limited to no more than 305 cubic inches.

Dodge engineers smoothed out some of the Charger's wrinkles for 1969 by moving the grille forward to a flush position and filling in the recessed backlight tunnel. They called the resulting new car the Charger 500 for obvious reasons. Here 500 pilot Bobby Isaac (#71) leads Charlie Glotzbach (#6) (also in a Charger 500) at Daytona in the second of the 1969 Twin Qualifiers for the 500. Isaac went on to win that race—the only superspeedway victory scored by a Charger 500 that year. Daytona Speedway Archives

With the stroke of a pen, the factory-backed aerowars were over. The final tally of superspeedway wins reads as follows: 14 for Talladega; eight for Spoiler II; seven for Superbird; six for Daytona and one for Charger 500. Though the winged Dodges and Plymouths fell short of their Ford and Mercury counterparts in the total number of mile-or-more wins raked up during the two-year factory-backed aerowars, they (and their street-going stablemates) are by far the most fondly remembered Grand National cars of the era.

The Charger 500 project began with pencil sketches that were then recreated in 3/8ths scale for wind tunnel testing. Author collection

Fomoco fired the first shots of the aerowars in 1968 when it introduced two all-new fastback rooflined intermediates. When those two new models ran off and left the equally new for 1968 Charger, the Charger 500 was born. Author collection

CHAPTER FOUR

1971: BIG BILL FRANCE PLUCKS THE WINGED CARS' FEATHERS

The significantly increased speeds made possible by the factory-built aerowarriors produced during the 1969 and 1970 seasons had caused NASCAR officials more than a few sleepless nights. While qualifying speed in the 200 mile per hour range and headline stealing hot laps like Buddy Baker's March 24, 1970, circuit of Talladega at 200.096 miles per hour were great for gate receipts, they raised significant concerns about safety at NASCAR's highest levels. Tech inspectors first addressed those concerns in August of 1970 with the introduction of flow restricting, horsepower robbing restrictor plates that were designed to trim top speeds. While that first ever use of those flow inhibitors had reined in superspeedway velocities somewhat, the NASCAR dons were not satisfied with the result. Something more would have to be done. For 1971 NASCAR officials decided to get even more serious about speed reduction by limiting all special aerobody cars to no more than 305 cubic inches.

Though Chryco's wing cars automatically became obsolete (with one notable exception),

The 1971 Charger turned out to be quite a successful race car. It also made a handsome street mount. Sometimes referred to as a coke bottle bodied car, the Charger was sleek and stylish.

Dodge and Plymouth drivers' collective fortunes were still improved for the upcoming season by the November 1970 announcement that Ford Motor Company was getting out of racing all together.

With the flow of factory dollars stopped, it was a sure bet that Fomoco drivers would be much less of an impediment to Chryco Grand National wins. As a result, Dodge and Plymouth drivers could hardly be blamed for expecting great things from the 1971 season.

With the winged cars that had so dominated the series in 1970 now (for the most part) sitting on the sidelines, most Chryco drivers elected to field more or less stock bodied Chargers and Satellites for 1971. Ray Elder, for example, scored first blood for Chrysler with a win at the season opener at Riverside earned in a stock bodied 1970 Charger.

Pete Hamilton made the new for 1971 Satellite body a winner with a twin qualifier victory at Daytona the Thursday before the 500. Buddy Baker came close to earning that same honor for the new coke bottle bodied 1971 Charger with a close second place (to David Pearson's Holman & Moody Mercury) finish in the second traditional speedweeks 125 miler. A.J. Foyt claimed the pole position for the 500 in the #21 Wood brothers

Mercury, but Bobby Isaac was just a heartbeat slower and his performance earned the #71 K&K 1971 Charger the outside pole on race day.

As mentioned, NASCAR rules for 1971 limited winged cars to just 305 cubic inches of displacement. As a result, most Chryco drivers opted to go wingless for the 1971 500—but not all. The lone exception was the Mario Rossi prepped Dodge Daytona that showed up at Daytona with a race-ready small block under its stretched bonnet. Driver Dick Brooks qualified the lone wing car a very respectable eighth on the field. When the green flag fell, the first 60 laps or so were dominated by big block powered cars as expect-

ed. But on lap 60, Brooks made fans in the stands rise to their feet and cheer when he pulled his #22 Daytona out in front to take the lead. He led again on lap 64 and yet another time on lap 98. Unfortunately, shortly after that last stint at the front, Brooks became involved in a fender bending shunt that upset his Daytona's aerodynamics and never led again. He still turned in a very respectable seventh place finish. That impressive run turned out to be the last competitive laps turned in by a Chryco winged car on the NASCAR tour.

Richard Petty earned his third Daytona 500 win that February day in 1971, and he did it in a conventionally configured 1971 Satellite race car.

Street Chargers continued to pack a Hemi punch into the seventies and the regular production status of that engine helped keep 426s legal in the NASCAR garage area. This particular car is the last Hemi Charger ever built. It belongs to Alabama's Doug Wellborn.

That triumph turned out to be the first of 21 Grand National wins scored for Plymouth by Petty that year. Along the way to the end of the 47 event 1971 season, Petty made visits to victory lanes at Richmond, Rockingham, North Wilkesboro, Martinsville, Atlanta, Richmond and Dover. When not in the lead that year, Petty wasn't very far off the pace as he finished in the top five fully 38 times. Petty's performance earned him more than $351,000 and his third Grand National driving title. Dodge drivers Bobby Isaac, Buddy Baker (in the Petty Enterprises Charger) and Bobby Allison added eight more wins to the Mopar total for 1971.

Though Ford and Mercury drivers claimed high profile superspeedway wins in the Atlanta 500, the Winston 500, the World 600, the Motor State 400, the Mason Dixon 500, the Talladega 500, the National 500 and the Southern 500, 1971 was still an exceptional year on the NASCAR circuit for Dodge and Plymouth drivers.

Petty's office during his Charger days was anything but plush. A single bucket seat kept him in place in the twisties and within easy reach of the Hurst shifter and steering wheel. Note how much less complex the 1970's style roll cage was than the safety assembly found on a modern cup car.

Richard Petty switched to Dodge late in the 1972 season not long after picking up STP as his primary sponsor. For the next five seasons his STP Chargers were the class of the field.

Though limited to a minuscule (by Daytona standards) 2-inch rear deck spoiler, Petty's Charger was plenty aerodynamic.

Unfortunately, it was the last year of Chrysler factory sponsored stock car competition.

1972
The Second Last Season for Plymouth Wins

1971 had seen the beginning of a move away from the 426 Hemi engine that had won so much glory for Dodge and Plymouth drivers since 1964. It was not a step that most teams took voluntarily. On the contrary, their collective decisions to eschew Hemi-headed big blocks in favor of conventional wedge-headed 426s was a move that had been coerced by the official NASCAR rules book. More specifically, by the late season rules change that saddled Hemi-headed engines with carburetors carrying throttle bores far smaller than the fuel mixers permitted for use on top of wedge-headed power plants. That same trend away from Hemi power continued into the 1972 season. All too soon, the low bellow of a full race 426 Hemi would be stilled forever.

Richard Petty and his Mopar compatriots went to war in 1972 at the helm of essentially the

Richard Petty recently called the Charger he raced from 1972 to 1977 his all-time favorite race car. And that should not come as a big surprise since they helped him win 37 Grand National events and two NASCAR championships. Author collection

same Satellites and Chargers they'd campaigned the year before. Like virtually every Dodge and Plymouth stocker built since 1964, those cars were built around unit body chassis and featured HD torsion bar suspension components at the bow and a leaf spring corporate 8 3/4-inch differential at the rear. Drum brakes were still part of the program in 1972 (though disc brakes would soon begin to show up in the Grand National garage area). Still incredibly stock by modern standards, the Mopar stock cars that qualified for competition in 1972 no longer carried full side glass or door trim like their sixties progenitors had. Treaded racing tires and production based rims had also become a thing of the past by 1972. And, as mentioned, big block

Richard Petty's last Mopar race car was this 1978 Dodge Magnum. Unfortunately it was an unlovely car with all of the aerodynamic aplomb of a brick. Petty never won a race in the car and in 1978 he decided to switch to GM. It was the end of an era for Mopar fans on the tour. Daytona Speedway Archives

By 1978 Dodge drivers like Robbins and Petty had switched to small block engines for power. Though Chryco racers had once relied on thunder Hemi engines for NASCAR work, by the late seventies, small block engines had made big inchers as extinct as the dodo bird.

Previous pages
Country and Western star Marty Robbins was one of several Dodge drivers who tried to make the Magnum body style work in stock car competition. Unfortunately he had no more success than the others. Mike Slade

racing engines were on the verge of extinction in both wedge and Hemi configuration.

As per usual, the 1972 season began with the road course Winston 500 at Riverside. Richard Petty captured that challenging event in convincing fashion in his still, all Petty Blue #43 Road Runner. A broken valve in the Daytona 500 one month later kept Petty from victory lane and mechanical gremlins also undid Dodge driver Bobby Isaac's pole winning performance during the race. A.J. Foyt's Wood brothers Cyclone was top dog at Daytona in 1972 and the best a Mopar driver could manage was the one lap down second place berth turned in by Charlie Glotzbach in a Cotton Owens built Charger.

Petty was back in victory lane one race later at Richmond, however, and Bobby Isaac scored the first 1972 win for Dodge at Rockingham in the Carolina 500 less than a month after that. Buddy Baker made superspeedway headlines at Charlotte in the World 600 where he led the last 30 laps of that grueling event in a Petty prepped #11 Dodge before taking the checkered flag

A number of Mopar stalwarts like Buddy Arrington continued to campaign Chryco race cars into the eighties. One of the last Mopar race cars to take to the high banks was this Chrysler Imperial that Arrington drove during the 1985 season. Mike Slade

In the late 1980s, a number of ARCA teams built and campaigned a gaggle of specially lengthened Chrysler LeBaron stock cars.

By the late eighties, NASCAR stock cars had lost all touch with their "stock" origins. Arrington's car carried a fabricated bucket seat, for example, and lacked just about any factory original "ergonomic" equipment.

When NASCAR officials scuttled plans for a winged version of the 1971 Road Runner, Richard Petty was forced to campaign a stock (more or less) bodied version of the car. Even so, he had a good season. Daytona Speedway Archives

Though the LeBarons were fast and showed promise, NASCAR officials refused to allow the cars to compete on the Winston Cup circuit.

first. Team owner Petty scored yet another superspeedway win in the Lone Star 500 at Texas World Speedway in June. Petty scored that win at the helm of a 1972 Plymouth, but his Mayflower division days had nearly come to an end. He'd shown up at Talladega in May with a Petty blue (and STP red) Dodge Charger. He'd also campaigned that same car in the World 600, the Mason Dixon 500 and the Motor State 400 before hopping back in his Plymouth. Petty was back in his Dodge for the Firecracker 400 and then switched back to the Road Runner at Bristol. He continued to alternate between the two marques for most of the rest of the season scoring Plymouth wins at Richmond, Martinsville and North Wilkesboro

and Dodge seconds at Daytona and Atlanta. In 1973 Petty switched exclusively to Dodge and his Plymouth days were over for good. Buddy Baker finished the season on a high note for Dodge fans by winning the season-closing Texas 500 in the K&K Charger.

Petty's eight Plymouth wins and 25 Plymouth and Dodge top five finishes earned him the 1972 Grand National crown. It turned out to be the last NASCAR championship ever won by a Plymouth driver. Sadly, there was to be but one more Plymouth Grand National victory—that being the win Dick Brooks scored in the 1973 Talladega 500. After that triumph, the light went out for Plymouth drivers on the Grand National (now Winston Cup) tour.

Richard Petty switched to Dodge Charger race cars late in 1972. He continued to campaign coke bottle bodied Dodges for the next five seasons. Today Petty remembers the cars as his favorite Grand National stock cars. Mike Slade

1973 Petty Does Dodge

In 1973 Petty shifted his automotive allegiance to Dodge full-time. That proved to be a wise move as over the next five seasons Petty used a series of sleek 426 wedge and 366ci small block motorvated coke bottle bodied Chargers to win 37 Grand National/Winston Cup events (including back-to-back Daytona 500s in 1973 & 1974) and two more national driving championships in 1974 and 1975.

When recently asked to name his all-time favorite NASCAR stock car, Petty quickly chose the Dodge Chargers he campaigned from 1972 to 1977. And it is easy to see why—they were incredible competition machines and they returned a series of legendary performances. In that number was the unforgettable 1976 Daytona finish that saw Petty and arch Fomoco rival David (the Silver Fox) Pearson hammer their way around the track on the last lap of the race, only

Dodge and Plymouth race cars continued to roll on torsion bar front suspension into the seventies. This is the setup used under Richard Petty's 1974 Charger, for example. Note the fabricated control arms and the drum brakes. Also note the wedge-headed 426 engine that Petty switched to when NASCAR's restrictor plate rule choked the life out of the 426 Hemi.

to crash within sight of the checkered flag. While Pearson claimed the win by limping his battered Wood brothers Mercury across the line ahead of Petty's equally savaged Charger, that finish still stands out in Mopar fans' memories today.

Though few realized it at the time, Neil Bonnet scored the final Dodge victory in NASCAR history in the last race of the 1977 season. The event in question was the then season-ending Los Angeles Times 500 held at the now defunct Ontario Motor Speedway (which, by the way, had been built as an exact replica of the Indianapolis Motor Speedway). After that victory, there was to be only darkness for Dodge drivers in stock car competition. Mopar partisans like Petty and Buddy Arrington tried to make a go of the Dodge Magnum body style that had to be used starting with the 1978 season, but that unlovely car was nothing less than an aerodynamic disaster. Another problem confronted by Mopar racers in the late seventies was the increasing difficulty they had finding suitable high-performance engine parts. Dodge and Plymouth had been out of the racing business for most of a decade by that time and the Chevrolet small block dominated aftermarket parts industry simply had not stepped in to fill the high performance void.

In 1978, Petty made one last attempt to build a competitive Mopar-based NASCAR car out of a Mirada body. But when testing proved that car to be no better than the bulky and unwieldy Magnum, Petty bit the bullet and switched to Chevrolet. When Petty roared beneath the green flag at the Champion Spark Plug 400 at Michigan on August 20, 1978, he was at the wheel of a Petty Blue Monte Carlo.

It was the end of an era. Though feisty independents like Buddy Arrington and Frank Warren would soldier on with Dodge and Chrysler based stockers into the eighties, the glory days of Mopar stock car racing were well and truly in the past. The official NASCAR records book today lists 190 all-time stock car wins for Plymouth drivers, 162 for the Dodge counterparts and 59 for Chrysler drivers.

Though the later eighties saw a number of ARCA teams build and campaign a handful of stretch bodied Chrysler Lebaron stock cars, NASCAR officials did not allow those cars to run in the Winston Cup series. Until and unless Chrysler once again builds a chassis that is adaptable to the modern Winston Cup rules book, there will be no more Mopar victories added to the impressive total scored between 1949 and 1977. And that is very sad indeed.

The ARCA LeBarons were all powered by high horsepower evolutions of the 360 small block engine. Note the restrictor plate that teams had to carry at Daytona.

INDEX